Here's What Clients Are Saying . . .

Strategies for closing the loop on communications make a lot of sense. Leaders who communicate up, down, and across organizational lines build credibility with customers and employees. It's about connecting with people, leading from the frontlines, not the sidelines, as Booher says. And the payoff is big.

—Ralph D. Heath
President
Lockheed Martin Aeronautics Company

Dianna Booher says very few people admit to being a poor communicator. The fact is, excellent communication skills are critical to effective leadership. The insights Dianna shares in this book are a must read for those few, as well as all the experts.

—Tim Minard
Senior Vice President
Principal Financial Group

For employees to be engaged in their work, they must trust their leaders. To build trust people must know you care, are competent and consistent. Communication is a core skill for every leader and it is essential to building trust within an organization. This book provides the reader with sound communication strategies"

—Deborah Masten
Vice President and
Director of Associate Development
JCPenney Company

Life is about relationships. And relationships are about communication. Dianna Booher takes the mystery out of communication skills.

—Dr. O. S. Hawkins
President and CEO
GuideStone Financial Resources
of the Southern Baptist Convention

This book outlines what's missing in most organizations today—clear communication! I hope leaders are listening . . . and reading it. Highly recommended.

—Kevin Connell
Vice President, Bell Helicopter XworX

Dianna Booher has taken her well-honed and world-class guidance on effective communication to a new, different, and powerful level. Without ever using the word, the book is about engagement. Companies are constantly trying to increase the level of employee engagement, knowing it can lead to improved business performance. In an easy-to-read style, this book makes it clear that leaders are at the front in this struggle and it lays out the behaviors and actions that help move the needle. It's about building personal credibility, openness, "touch," and trust as a leader—all keys to unlocking the potential of the people you lead. Take her "final notes" page and put it to use every day—your organization will be stronger and more vital for it.

—John W. Gill
Executive Vice President, Human Resources
Rolls-Royce North America, Inc.

THE VOICE
OF
AUTHORITY

10 Communication Strategies Every Leader Needs to Know

Dianna Booher

McGraw-Hill

New York   Chicago   San Francisco   Lisbon   London
Madrid   Mexico City   Milan   New Delhi
San Juan   Seoul   Singapore
Sydney   Toronto

1 2 3 4 5 6 7 8 9 0   DOC/DOC   0 9 8 7

ISBN-13: 978-0-07-148669-9
ISBN-10:0-07-148669-0

This publication is designed to provide accurate and authoritative informa-tion in regard to the subject matter covered. It is sold with the understanding that the publisher is not engaged in rendering legal, accounting, or other pro-fessional service. If legal advice or other expert assistance is required, the serv-ices of a competent professional person should be sought.
  —From a declaration of principles jointly adopted by a committee of the American Bar Association and a committee of publishers.

McGraw-Hill books are available at special quantity discounts to use as pre-miums and sales promotions, or for use in corporate training programs. For more information, please write to the Director of Special Sales, Professional Publishing, McGraw-Hill, Two Penn Plaza, New York, NY 10121-2298. Or contact your local bookstore.

Library of Congress Cataloging-in-Publication Data

Booher, Dianna Daniels.
    The voice of authority / by Dianna Booher.
        p. cm.
    Includes bibliographical references and index.
    ISBN 0-07-148669-0 (alk. paper)
  1. Communication in management. 2. Leadership. I. Title.
    HD30.3.B664 2007
    658.4'5—dc22

                                                            2007000671

Contents

Acknowledgments

I want to express my heartfelt thanks to several on the Booher team who've contributed significantly to this book: Sally Luttrell, Chris Casady, Jacque Hocking, and Mark Bilgere for their help with the Booher Communication Survey; Rachel Rhodes for compiling survey results and helping prepare the manuscript; Candy Wright for compiling survey results and helping with research; and Polly Fuhrman for help in copyediting and manuscript preparation.

I also wish to thank Glen Sheppard for help with research, creating graphics, and reading the manuscript and offering suggestions; Vernon Rae for reading the manuscript and offering suggestions; my editor, Donya Dickerson, and all the team at McGraw-Hill for their enthusiastic support for this project, as well as my past books published with them; and my agent, Doris Michaels, for her optimism and support in all my writing projects.

Finally, I want to thank you, loyal readers and clients, who so graciously have shared your stories through the years. Those experiences add significantly to our projects together, make our work meaningful, and enrich our lives.

Dianna Booher

THE VOICE
OF
AUTHORITY

There Is Just No Communication around Here

*How people talk to each other
absolutely determines how well the
organization will function.*
—Larry Bossidy, Chairman,
Honeywell International

D o you have a boss who demands rather than asks? Do you have suppliers who promise but don't deliver? Do you have a spouse who growls rather than responds? Do you have a child who explodes rather than expresses feelings?

Whether at home or in your workplace, poor communication is often the culprit. A common complaint: "There's just no communication around here!"

What could people possibly mean by that comment? With paper swirling on every desk, e-mail in-boxes overflowing, a cell phone in every hand, what do people mean by "no communication"? What does your boss, coworker, or mother-in-law mean by that comment? What do *you* mean by that comment? But wait. Before you answer that question, consider the following situation:

Jorge walks out of a big presentation to the senior executives and turns to his boss, who is leading the project team. "Well, how did you think it went in there?"

The manager says to him, "Nice job. You nailed it."

A month later, Jorge is terminated. Reason stated: Lacks understanding of big-picture goals and how his projects align with those goals. Where did the miscommunication happen? Did Jorge's manager just not give him the straight truth about a bad presentation? Was Jorge's manager off base in her understanding of the meeting dynamics and feedback? Or had the executives failed to communicate their goals clearly from the beginning?

Companies lose employees and customers every week because they can't teach people to communicate clearly and candidly with each other. Period. It's that simple. And that complex.

Your Opportunity to Lead

This is where you come in—that is, your answer to the earlier question: What makes people complain, "There's just no communication around here"? If you can answer that question—and do something about it—you can be heard. You can create conversation. You can change things.

The answer is not about technology. Blogging, instant-messaging, text-messaging, smart phones—all, just like e-mail and faxes, will be passé after a few years. New technology appears and disappears from the scene. The one constant is *human* communication.

Your career opportunity is your ability to use the principles of effective human communication to create connections and make things happen.

How do you know if you're any good as a communicator? By the results you get—or don't get. You either clarify or confuse. You either motivate or demoralize. You either gain buy-in or generate distrust.

Symptoms of Poor Personal Communication

Most of us think we're excellent communicators. Unfortunately, our own understanding or response is not the best measure of effectiveness. Everything we say is clear to us—or we wouldn't have said it that way. So when we look outward for clues of poor communication, these symptoms often surface:

- ▶ Feeling that everyone agrees with and supports what you say, feel, and do most of the time
- ▶ Lack of input, questions, or feedback on your ideas presented in meetings
- ▶ Few or no ideas contributed in your meetings
- ▶ Inability to influence others to accept your ideas or change their viewpoint or behavior
- ▶ Seeing little or no behavioral change in people you've coached for improved performance
- ▶ Confusion about what you're supposed to be doing
- ▶ Lack of understanding the "why" behind assigned projects and goals
- ▶ Thinking that what you do or say doesn't really "change things" in the long run
- ▶ Nervousness or hesitancy about presenting new ideas to your boss, client, or strategic partners
- ▶ Ongoing conflict with peers or family
- ▶ Frequent rework

- Constant reminders from you to others to take action, meet deadlines, or send information
- Frequent requests for more information about topics or issues that you think you've already addressed sufficiently
- Feeling of disconnection and discomfort in one-on-one and small-group interactions
- Lack of positive feedback about your presentations or documents (from those not obligated to give it)

Symptoms of Poor Communication in Your Organization

Again, ask executives if their organizations communicate well and chances are you'll hear a resounding yes. But ask those a little lower in the ranks and you may hear otherwise. These symptoms crop up:

- Conflicting goals and objectives (Susan wants to cut costs; Sam wants to increase revenue.)
- Conflicting priorities (Su Lin wants her sales staff trained before they get in front of customers; Dupree wants his staff in front of customers as soon as possible, with or without all the obligatory training.)
- Conflicting schedules
- Left-hand, right-hand blindness (Division A doesn't know what Division B is doing and often duplicates—or complicates—their work.)
- Turf wars
- Unclear values
- Low morale; people doing just enough to "get by"

- Lack of coordination of routine tasks; details "falling between the cracks"
- Rework
- Gossip, rumors
- "Us" against "them" attitudes and conversations
- Poor team "chemistry" (either open expressions of hostility or silent withdrawal and cynicism)
- Jargon and "double-speak" between departments

How Did We Sink to This State of Affairs?

The "Spray and Pray" Mentality

One of the three biggest communication challenges, according to directors of communications, is getting senior executives to pay more than lip service to the idea. Shellye Archambeau, CEO of a technology firm called Metric-Stream, uses the "spray and pray" phrase to label executives who shower people with information and hope they can make sense of it, thus creating the illusion that everyone is informed.

In my own consulting practice, I've yet to discover a senior executive who doesn't say that "people are our most valuable asset" and "communication is vital to our success."

But when feedback from an employee survey reveals communication breakdowns, these same executives scratch their heads: "What are they talking about? We bombard them with information! It's on the intranet. It's on the Web. We had a teleconference on that issue last Thursday. They have an 800 number to call. We have monthly staff meetings. I don't see how we could possibly give people more information. What do they want?"

> *Information is not communication. Information is not a message. Information is not a connection. Information does not translate to execution. Information does not drive sales or profits. The difference between information and communication is the difference between an X-ray and surgery.*

Information is not communication. Information is not a message. Information is not a connection. Information does not translate to execution. Information does not drive sales or profits. The difference between information and communication is the difference between an X-ray and surgery. Leaders understand the difference between the volume of communication and its significance.

Gurus Repackaging the Old as the "New"

Professors, consultants, and others out to make a name for themselves by selling new "models" have to repackage ideas continually. We humans come by the habit naturally. Check any collection of quotations and you'll find that what Aristotle, the Apostle Paul, or John Adams said has been rephrased by rock stars, pro athletes, and corporate leaders through the years.

The problem: Repackaging typically calls for more complex labels and language. So people tune out with "heard it all before."

"Spin" Spotting

Our psyche filters out messages that first come to us. We're schooled to "sniff for the stink," "wait for the other shoe to fall," "wait until the dust settles," or "wait for the air to clear" before getting the true story.

Here is how we typically respond to what we hear:

1. Hear the situation and/or facts.
2. Wait for the spin.
3. Download the intentions.
4. Decode the spin.

To make the process faster, we tune out until step 3. In short, we listen defensively, skeptically—as if everything we're hearing is half-truth with a hidden motive behind the spin.

Risk-Averse Culture: "Not I," Said the Little Red Hen

Nobody wants to claim responsibility or be accountable for actions or decisions. The situation has worsened during the last 25 years that my company has been offering training in business writing. In the 1980s, as part of a two-day workshop, we taught participants how to respond to customer complaints. Only occasionally did we encounter a company that didn't allow their service agents to respond to complaints at all—but instead, because of liability concerns, required them to pass that task on to supervisors. Today, the task is handled almost universally by managers. Why? Fear of having service agents say, "We made a mistake."

The same thing happens internally in the most minor situations. People create an unending number of obscure e-mails to avoid saying, "I'm accountable, and I made a mistake."

Turning Communication into a Template

Another communication killer is the overuse of templates, which turns people into drones and clones without personality or voice. Templates remove the thought process. Templates tend to dehumanize and generalize communication.

Of course I'm speaking metaphorically. But I'm also speaking literally.

There's a growing trend to standardize all presentations so that everyone using PowerPoint must use the same template (typically with the heading in the same spot, bullet points, and a "take-away" at the bottom). At trade shows, meeting planners often send out templates to conference speakers, suggesting that they dump all their slides into the standard template so they all have the same "look and feel." Often, corporate communication directors mandate such in the name of "branding." Is it any wonder we're now hearing complaints about "death by PowerPoint" as if the tool is the problem?

Customer relationship management (CRM) software systems generate template e-mails and letters to respond to customers—responses that rarely answer the customers' specific questions.

The whole world is trying to communicate by template. The call center hears "Problem X," so they send e-mail D response. The doctor hears symptoms Y and Z, so the pharmacy spits out the printed warnings and side effects along with the prescriptions. The customer from the food service industry calls, so the sales team delivers Standard Sales Presentation ABC.

Result: No one connects. Everything is general. Nothing stands out. All seems irrelevant. Most gets ignored.

Obnoxious Behavior—Courtesy of Anonymity

Have you ever had someone keep you waiting to continue a conversation while they repeatedly answered their phone? Or how about "no reply" bravado when you e-mail someone with a direct question: "Can you have the report to me by Friday before Bill's retirement get-together at 3:00?" They respond, "Good thing you reminded me of the party. I'll see you at 3:00." They never answer the question about the report—intentionally.

Thanks to the Internet, people feel anonymous as long as they're not eyeball-to-eyeball with you.

Political Correctness

Similar problems occur when people are afraid that direct communication may hurt someone's feelings. People will put up with bad language, bad attitudes, and bad performance from their team members, clients, and coworkers all in the name of political correctness. They fear being labeled prejudiced against a certain ethnic group, age group, or gender. Managers often rely on e-mail notices or the Human Resources representative to have the tough conversations with their employees.

In fact, some people dread a straightforward conversation so much (whether because they themselves are uncomfortable or because the other person is defensive or easily crushed) that they hire an outsider to deal with the problem. People can even hire anonymous individuals on the Internet for a small fee (www.GentleHints.com) to let a coworker, boss, or neighbor know they wear too much perfume, make lousy presentations, or have parties that are too loud.

Executives and boards of directors hire consultants to have similar conversations.

The Herd Mentality

Bad models—leaders, documents, presentations, speeches, meeting agendas, facilitators—exist everywhere. People feel safer if they communicate "like everyone else." Different draws attention. Same is secure.

Your Golden Career Opportunity: Clear Up the Communication Clutter

According to the late Peter Drucker, writing in the *Harvard Business Review,* summarizing his 65-year consulting career with CEOs, one of the eight key tenets of effective executives is taking responsibility for communication. Leaders lead; they take responsibility for the communication culture. Managers maintain; they go with the status quo.

Leaders become the face or human connection of an organization. They "connect" with other people—coworkers, clients, partners, each other—to get things done. Specifically, they communicate values. They act consistently with those values. They communicate respect and concern. They tell the truth.

What's the payoff to the organization?

The latest annual Watson Wyatt Communication ROI Study substantiates that companies with effective communication practices have a 19 percent higher market premium and a 57 percent higher shareholder return over five years than companies with ineffective communication practices. That potential payoff is too promising to ignore.

If your team, department, organization, or family doesn't change a negative communication culture, chances are great that it's going down the tubes sooner or later. Larry Bossidy and Ram Charan, authors of the bestseller *Execution: The Discipline of Getting Things Done*, cite example after example of company failures due to poor execution—and much of it can be traced to poor internal communication. A few years ago, *Fortune* magazine also explored why companies fail. Of the 10 reasons cited, four centered on dysfunctional communication—"see no evil, dysfunctional board, fearing the boss, dangerous corporate culture."

If you have to work in this kind of dysfunctional culture, you can be the miracle worker. Clearing up fuzzy communication will have a huge impact on your team's success.

What's the payoff personally? You'll be able to

▶ Identify what to communicate, when to communicate it, and how to say it so that it sticks.

▶ Create compelling conversations to influence others to act.

▶ Connect with people to increase trust and cooperation.

▶ Facilitate understanding in complex, controversial, and difficult situations.

▶ Encourage information sharing rather than information hoarding.

▶ Build morale, improve team chemistry, and make others feel part of the group.

▶ Increase your credibility and impact when speaking before a group.

- ▶ Make others' work meaningful to them.
- ▶ Be able to coach others to improve their performance.

But hold on a moment before we sing "Kumbaya." You're not going to accomplish this miracle overnight— without answering the earlier question.

What do people—your boss, your cube mate, your kids—mean by the comment, "There's just no communication around here!" What makes people think that others aren't giving them correct, clear, complete information? Why does that perception become reality? Why do the people in Sales not talk to the people in Customer Service? Why does the first shift forget to tell the second shift that Machine 286 needs cleaning before it blows up?

On the other hand, why do people keep sending data, graphs, slides, and e-mail, thinking they're communicating? Why do parents keep talking "till they're blue in the face" and never get their kids to tune in?

> *What we've got here is . . . a failure to communicate!*
>
> —CAPTAIN,
> COOL HAND LUKE

Okay, seven questions rather than one. But they're all linked.

Ten Reasons People Resist What You Say— and What You Can Do about It

People typically reject what they hear for one of the following reasons or perceptions:

- ▶ They think you're lying or misleading them. They don't trust you.

- They're getting incomplete information.

- They don't understand what you mean. Your message is unclear.

- You're being purposefully evasive—with either good or wrong intentions.

- What you're saying seems inconsistent with what you're doing.

- They don't consider you credible—either you don't look or talk the part or they don't like you.

- They think you don't care about them personally. They don't feel a connection with you.

- You're slow to communicate. They've heard important information from somebody else—and they feel "done wrong" because you didn't tell them first.

- They think you're incompetent in your job because of weak communication skills.

- They're working in isolation, with no opportunity for input or feedback.

Each chapter in this book will tackle one of these basic challenges and present strategies for successfully "getting through" to people despite these feelings and situations. You'll discover ways either to prevent the reality or change the perception that "there's just no communication around here."

For example, these strategies will help you decide when to communicate. Before you have all the facts? In the middle of investigating a problem or incident? After you've made a final decision? Before you know where people stand on an issue?

You'll also identify what to communicate. What do people need to know to do their jobs well? Why do people

> *Leaders understand the difference between the volume of communication and its significance.*

consider such information essential? Why do people withhold information from each other? How do you encourage cross-functional communication and create compelling conversations?

Finally, you'll consider how best to communicate both routine and sensitive messages—and the difference that structure, phrasing, timing, connection, and context make to getting others to accept your ideas and cooperate to make things happen.

And if you're already communicating well, congratulations. In that case, use these strategies to solidify relationships when the inevitable crisis occurs. Until then, continue to communicate with confidence®, knowing that's the key to a productive, engaged team that gets things done.

CHAPTER 1

Is It Correct?

The statement has truth but not quite enough to be true.

—Francis M. Cornford

Giving my deposition proved to be one of the most depressing days of my life. Like Dorothy waking up in the Land of Oz, I realized I wasn't in Kansas anymore.

My husband and I had bought a piece of property on which the previous owner hadn't disclosed that it was located in a creek floodway (meaning it could never be reclaimed and built on). Neither did the Realtor® representing both of us, the buyer and seller in the transaction, investigate the issue as we had asked her to do. So when we discovered we'd paid a king's ransom for practically worthless land, we were forced to file a lawsuit against the landowner and Realtor for their nondisclosure.

Here's what I expected at the deposition from the owner and Realtor: a lot of "he said/she said." Or, "When you asked about X, I thought you meant Y." Or, "When I said Z, what I really meant was B." And a plethora of, "I don't remember," "I don't recall," "I don't know," and maybe some confusion on dates and details.

What I *didn't* expect was this. When we had half a dozen meetings, I didn't expect the Realtor to say that we had only two. When we'd walked through the house with the Realtor on four occasions, I didn't expect her to say that we'd never been inside the house. When we'd asked the Realtor repeatedly to investigate the floodplain situation, I didn't expect her to say the issue "had never come up." Since the property flooded every time there was a heavy rain, I didn't expect the landowner to say he "forgot" his property was in a floodway.

As I later recounted the experience to an attorney friend, his response was not exactly comforting. "I'm a criminal lawyer. I see it happen every day with police officers and public officials where there are no witnesses. Every day." It was one of the most emotionally draining two days of my life.

Lying at work has the same effect. Spin drains us and enrages us. The truth, the whole truth, and nothing but the truth . . . should not be three different things.

The Climate

Can You Keep All the Plates, . . . er . . . Leaders, Spinning?

The challenge used to be keeping all the plates spinning. Now the challenge seems to be keeping all the leaders spinning. Spin drives our businesses and our lives. Spin means putting the best face on a situation, stating facts or the situation in the best light possible—to get a date, to close a deal, to gain support for a cause, to solicit money for charity, to change a philosophical viewpoint.

Spin happens—according to whatever point you're trying to put forward and according to your own biases. (There's ethical and unethical spin, of course. But more about that later.)

Recently, in my blog (http://booherbanter.typepad.com) I wrote about the spin each TV network gave the story of Al-Zarqawi's death in Iraq. Some of the comments heard the morning after on various morning network shows:

- ▶ "It's a great victory for the U.S. this morning."
- ▶ "His death will have little real effect on the war in Iraq."
- ▶ "It's only a psychological victory."
- ▶ "It's a great symbolic victory."
- ▶ "I think we'll begin to see things improve substantially now in Iraq."
- ▶ "His death will certainly boost Bush's ratings at home."
- ▶ "But we need to do a reality check on how little his death will really affect Bush's ratings here at home."
- ▶ "Al-Zarqawi was the most recognizable terrorist name in Iraq."
- ▶ "Al-Zarqawi was nothing more than a street thug who knew how to use the media—others behind the scenes control the real power."

Biases and emotions have a way of working their way to the surface of most conversations. If you want an intriguing pastime while waiting in line at the airport or grocery store, try decoding people's language to see what you can learn about their underlying assumptions and belief systems.

Spin is natural. We all spin. Otherwise, we'd never get a

date, a spouse, an employee, an employer, or a contract. We put our best foot forward.

Sinister spin is the problem.

Good Spin Gains Advantage

Good spin—

▶ Is grounded in reality and not misleading
▶ Is appropriate for the audience, time, and purpose
▶ Gives straight answers
▶ Serves the good intentions of the spinner

Sinister Spin Destroys Us

Sinister spin—

▶ Exaggerates, misleads, distorts, or covers up
▶ Shows bad taste—upsets people because it's delivered to an inappropriate audience, at the wrong time, for an ulterior purpose
▶ Destroys people's ability to trust and get a straight answer

Words sometimes serve as a smokescreen to obscure the truth, rather than as a searchlight to reveal it.

—ANONYMOUS

As a result of our "spinning" culture, corporations get caught up in the same habit. And employees and customers become equally skeptical. Even though sinister spin gets around the organization or the world at warp speed, thanks to the Internet, thinking people pull sinister spin apart. This couldn't be correct or true. There's an obvious bias and underlying motive here. That's an invalid conclusion. Somebody's not shooting straight with me on this issue.

Trust totters at an all-time low.

So Where Does the Spin Stop and the Scam Begin?

Walk into your office any Tuesday morning and your jammed e-mail box contains messages with subject lines that read "RE: Follow-up to Friday's Discussion." You click it open to learn that a barrister in Nigeria wants to deposit $40 million into your account. Another subject line from Jennifer. "Will you be able to attend trade show?" Click it open to discover you've been approved for a mortgage.

This is the culture in which you and I communicate.

According to a study done by the Pew Research Center for the People and the Press, people no longer believe what they read in the most prominent publications. Here's the breakdown of what percentage of people believe what they read and where:

Wall Street Journal: 41%
Time: 29%
Newsweek: 24%
USA Today: 23%

In a study done by the International Association of Business Communicators (IABC) Research Foundation, more than half of American workers reported observing ethical misconduct on the job. Lying to employees, customers, vendors, or the public was the second most often reported offense.

The lying issue goes from the bottom all the way to the top in organizations—from resumes and job interviews to options backdating. And the Securities and Exchange Commission (SEC) is cracking down. They have sent hundreds of letters to companies demanding that they tell the unvarnished truth to the public—to tell the story behind the numbers, to highlight any facts that could have a significant impact on the company's financials. After seeing their peers and competitors hauled off to jail or slapped with heavy fines, many have cleared the rising lump in their collective throats, neither admitted nor denied wrongdoing in their vague annual reports, and decided to settle out of court and pay fines.

Politicians parse truth no better—from Nixon to Clinton. You recall the Clinton classic in his Grand Jury testimony about the meaning of *is*:

> **Attorney:** Whether or not Mr. Bennet knew of your relationship with Ms. Lewinsky, the statement that there was "no sex of any kind in any manner, shape or form, with President Clinton," was an utterly false statement. Is that correct?
>
> **Clinton:** It depends upon what the meaning of the word *is* is. If . . . *is* means 'is and never has been and is not'—that is one thing. If it means there is none, that was a completely true statement.

In a press release dated April 25, 2002, announcing a 96 cents per share loss, Dennis Kozlowski, then CEO of Tyco International, had this to say: "I am disappointed that our ten-year/forty-quarter string of consistent earnings improvements has been broken. While our results before charges are in line with our previously stated expectations for the quarter, we met those expectations with a lower tax rate for the quarter." He never used the word *losses*. Sinister spinning becomes habit-forming, I suppose, considering Mr. Kozlowski's later prison sentence.

Your challenge as a communicator is to regain trust in a culture "spinning" out of control.

The Causes

Customer Promises and "All Best Wishes"

I walked into my neighborhood sports shop a few months back to buy some jogging shorts. I knew what I wanted—but not where to locate the item. The first clerk greeted me robotically as I entered his department. "May I help you?" I told him what I wanted. "That's not our department. Try across the aisle." He pointed.

I walked across the aisle. After a moment, I walked back into his department. "It seems there's no one in that department. Could you help me locate those running shorts?"

He sighed and followed me across the aisle. "I don't work over here. Let me find someone."

He brought a manager in tow. "Yes?" she said, "May I help you?"

I told her the type and style number of the shorts I wanted.

"All we have are over there on that rack."

She turned back to her inventory counting. I gave it a cursory look, walked out, and went home to order on the Internet from a different company.

"May I help you?" has become an insincere offer in far too many organizations. Customers smell it.

Individual Insincerities

Flattery makes it difficult to enjoy the real commendations that come our way. When introduced to someone senior in an organization, a common comment that rolls off the tongue is "You're a real role model." Have you ever had occasion to hear that executive respond with "Oh? In what way?" The flatterer tap dances trying to compose something sensible since he could write all he knows of the person on his thumbnail.

Such insincere comments are all part of the spin, spam, and smiles that make civility possible—but create a crisis of trust personally.

Management Clichés That Skirt the Truth

Several times a year, I address audiences of HR professionals. During those programs, attendees have the opportunity to share (anonymously, of course) untruths told in their organizations—those that they can verify because of their being privy to confidential information and conversations with senior executives. Here are the backstories—mentioned most often:

- ▶ "No one is going to lose their job when the merger happens." (Reality: Plans are already under way to lay off redundant departments.)
- ▶ "No one is getting a raise this year." (Reality: Senior executives are getting huge bonuses.)
- ▶ "We are all doing our part to cut expenses this year." (Reality: Offsite meetings, travel, bonuses, and perks for lower-ranking people are eliminated; no such changes are made for top executives.)

- "People are our most valuable asset." (Reality: But we don't trust them, train them, or listen to them.)
- "Training is a high priority." (Reality: We just don't want to pay for it or allow time off for it.)
- "You'll be better off under the new pay/benefit structure." (Reality: The company will be better off, so you can keep your job a while longer.)

Is it any wonder these organizations find themselves struggling to restore trust, retain employees, and realize objectives?

Flashes of Reality about Raymond

Everybody may love Raymond—but they also know when he's not pulling his weight. When people see Raymond goof off and hear that he got the same percentage raise as they did, they understand that "pay for performance" is a lie. When they do less than their best on their own projects and still receive the same praise and perks as everyone else, they understand that performance reviews have no basis in reality.

When employees realize that competitions such as Employee of the Month are restricted with rules that say awards can't go to the same person twice, they chalk up the whole concept as a ploy to get everybody to work a little harder with no real recognition for those who make a significant contribution month after month.

Off-Stage Lying: You, Me, and the Rest of Us

We lose trust when someone lies in our presence—even if not to us specifically. For example, you overhear your boss lie to a strategic partner about the percentage on commissions other partners receive. You see your client attend an industry conference paid for by his employer, skip out of all the sessions to play golf with an

old friend, and call the home office about how light the traffic has been "on the trade show floor" all day. You know your boss caused a major foul-up that delayed a project— yet on the monthly report to the vice president, she chalks up the delay to "supplier problems."

Off-stage lying—even when you're not the victim— causes questions about other things you hear.

Customer promises that don't pan out, individual insincerity, management clichés that don't ring true, off-stage lying—these obstacles make it tough to build trust. Is it any wonder that people trust the Internet for their information more often than their leaders?

The Cure

Tell the Truth: It's the Cover-Up, Not the Foul-Up, That's the Screw-Up in the End

Ask Richard Nixon, Bill Clinton, Martha Stewart, Pete Rose, Andrew Fastou, Jack Abramoff. Tell it like it is. When you're wrong, say so. When you make a mistake, step up to the plate. When you miss a deadline, own up. When you make a lousy decision, don't hide behind a committee, board, or team. When the outcome is disappointing, say so.

Nothing makes people believe you when you're right

like admitting when you're wrong. Nothing earns more respect than seeing someone's confidence in owning up to their blunders, decisions, or poor performance.

Trust builds over time. It can be dashed in a flash. It repairs slowly.

There's tremendous power in being known as a person who tells the truth. Straight. Unvarnished. Direct.

Give Your Spin the Cartoon Query

Yes, you'll want to put your best foot forward. But translate your values, beliefs, behavior, mission, or goals into concrete language. If it rolls off your tongue, chances are it's clichéd. Give it the Cartoon Query. Can you picture Scott Adams doing a Dilbert cartoon with your comment as the punch line? If so, rethink your announcement, explanation, or message so that it rings true.

Hold Others Accountable

Saying that you reward stellar performance, but continuing to coddle nonperforming Raymond because you love him becomes a thinly veiled lie. Set goals and standards. Communicate the criteria or what you plan to count. Measure. Quantify. Reward—or penalize—accordingly. Do what you say you will about others' performance.

Measure Perception as if It Were Reality— Follow the Smoke

A defiant 15-year-old in an emotional outburst slings this comment over her shoulder: "I don't care what others think about me." Inside, she's crying, "Of course I care what others think about me!"

Maturity brings the realization that what people think matters a great deal. Perception—rarely reality about the capability of candidates—determines the outcome of our presidential races. Perception—rarely reality of needs—determines the funds collected for charitable causes. Perception—rarely reality of guilt or innocence—determines the judgment and penalties in civil lawsuits.

Wise communicators do reality checks often. They realize that where there's smoke, there's usually a spark. The goal is to stomp on the spark before it becomes a bonfire.

The Soul and Substance of Truth-Telling

Trust builds over time. It can be dashed in a flash. It repairs slowly.

Not telling the truth proves stressful. Evasion and equivocation require energy. You have to remember what you said . . . to whom . . . during what time period. Then you have to wonder who heard it and how you phrased it, . . . worry what happens if someone else finds out, . . . and wonder who else actually understood it and read between the lines.

Every day we interact with bosses, customers, suppliers, coworkers, kids, spouses, or neighbors in sensitive situations with difficult questions. There are easy

There are easy answers. And then there are truthful, more difficult answers. Your power as a communicator often depends on the choice between the two.

answers. And then there are truthful, more difficult answers.

Your power as a communicator often depends on the choice between the two.

CHAPTER 2

Is It Complete?

*People will connect the dots in the
most pathological way possible.*
— Jeanie Daniel Duck
The Change Monster

Leaders often get so busy analyzing, problem solving,
questioning, coordinating, deciding, and delegating
that they fail to communicate what's going on to
those standing on the sidelines. They tell too little too late.
And in the absence of information, people get their facts
from whatever faucet is leaking—whether accurate or not.

As a leader, your silence doesn't mean the conversation
stops; it just means you have no input.

Pop quiz here:

▶ In the first 24, 48, or 72 hours after the terrorist attack on 9/11/2001, where did you spend all of your
waking hours? (In front of the TV?)

▶ Where was your attention during hurricanes Katrina
and Rita? (Listening to TV or radio or reading Internet updates?)

▶ How frequently do you read or listen to the details of
a scandal, death, or murder case that has nothing to

do with you—such as Scott and Laci Peterson? Jon-Benet Ramsey? Natalie Holloway? Steve Irwin? The Amish schoolchildren? Anna Nicole Smith? (Often?)

If your answers agreed with the ones in parentheses, congratulations—you're part of the human race. The hunger for details is a natural reaction. So when leaders withhold details—consciously or unconsciously—about things as important as our work, they generate anger, confusion, and disbelief.

Good communicators can't be cavalier about giving complete information.

Why People Skimp on the Details

Leave-the-Thinking-to-Us Mentality

Some teams, departments, and organizations have a paternalistic culture. The senior executives view run-of-the-mill employees as the children of the organization, not to be trusted with the real facts, information, and explanations about decisions or actions.

On various occasions, they take these different stances: "We'll let you know if something becomes important, so just don't worry about it." "We don't want to upset you with this news—maybe it'll go away without your ever having to hear about it." Or, "This is a very complex problem—much too involved for you to understand."

Whether the effort is well intentioned or not, such culture typically chokes people. They have no chance for input or feedback on the ideas or decisions. When their creativity is limited, morale goes down. And without the details, buy-in is limited. People don't have the logic that supports announced decisions.

Everybody seems to know the toy's broken—except the parent at the top.

The Power of Being the Only One "in the Know"

Saddam Hussein serves as an extraordinary example here. He hobbled his own military in their ability to fight external threats because he kept them in the dark about key information. According to the U.S. military reports and interviews, Saddam's military leaders were stunned and demoralized to learn only three months before the war that he had no weapons of mass destruction. They had counted on these hidden stockpiles for their nation's defense. He blocked communication among military leaders, and insisted that all commanders move troops only with his permission from Baghdad. The Fedayeen's operations were not shared with the leaders of the conventional forces. Neither did he allow the Republican Guard divisions to communicate with their sister units. Commanders couldn't even get precise maps of the terrain near the Baghdad airport for fear they'd be able to identify Iraqi leaders' palaces.

Sound like anyone who runs a project in your organization?

On one of my client visits, I heard about the White Knight. A coworker of his explained this way: "We'll be working on a client project—10 steps for installation of a client's software. He'll tell our consultants involved only eight of the steps. Then when they can't get the project to fly, the White Knight comes in at the last minute with the missing information and saves the day. He does this repeatedly. He has created huge animosity among the team. . . . Many very good people are looking for another job."

A CEO who recently sold his company has this story to tell about one of his acquisitions: "We acquired a company from a different industry. The sales manager there had been with the company for many, many years and could have helped us a lot by giving us information such as highlighting top customers to go after and the right products to pitch. We thought it was that kind of information we were buying when we acquired his company. But the sales manager thought if he 'doled it out slowly' to us that we'd need him more, that his job would be more secure. It was just the reverse. We finally gave up and went around him."

> *People withhold details to gain power. They lose it for the same reason.*

People withhold details to gain power. They lose it for the same reason.

Behind-the-Scenes Stuff and Fluff

Some people sail through the day or week unaware of what others need to know to do their job. Their thinking: "What does *my* X information have to do with *their* Y process?"

Long before the movie or TV show, "six degrees of separation" was a hypothesis set forth in 1929 by Hungarian writer Karinthy Frigyes. The theory holds that anybody on earth can be connected to any other person on the planet through a chain of acquaintances with no more than five intermediaries. That is, you know somebody, who knows somebody else, who knows somebody else. . . . Well, you get the picture. With six introductions, you could be connected to anybody you'd like to meet.

Although the theory has been tested through the years

but never proved, the point is this: If you so much as sneeze in your department, sooner or later it affects somebody else—their pocketbook, paperwork, process, or priorities.

Imagine this: You're an engineering manager working in Orlando and have been given orders to fly to New York City to head up a project team to build a sky bridge in the heart of Manhattan. You get halfway there and your cell phone rings, and your boss tells you to forget the sky bridge and head for San Diego. You've been assigned a new project—to construct new habitats for more than 20 percent of the animals in the San Diego Zoo.

You reschedule your flight and head for San Diego, leaving a five-minute broadcast voice mail for your staff to let them know of the change in mission, timelines, supplies needed, and staff assignments. Would you be concerned about what you might find waiting for you in San Diego to support the new project? How do you think the sudden change in mission might affect others' priorities, schedules, shipments, support activities for the week?

Supervisors do the equivalent of the bridge-to-zoo switch frequently, without letting staff or other departments know what's happening, why it's happening, or how it'll affect them.

Yet when leaders turn on a dime and communicate the details to all involved, employees will engage.

Too Busy to Make Things Easier

You've heard people say they're too busy to go to a time management class to get their life under control. So they remain disorganized and frantic. Similarly, some people claim they're too busy to communicate. Consequently, they waste time in cleaning up the mess of miscommunication—settling conflicts, clarifying misunderstood missions, rewriting unclear documents, rehashing the same old issues in unproductive meetings, and shuffling priorities and missed deadlines due to misunderstood directions.

Fear of Giving Bad News and Handling Negative Reactions

The world watched TV coverage of the behavior and communication from the Iraqi Information Minister, Muhammed Saeed al-Sahhaf, and President Saddam Hussein during the initial liberation effort and drive into Baghdad.

As American armored divisions launched assaults on Saddam International Airport 20 kilometers from the center of Baghdad and U.S.-led coalition troops advanced on the blacked-out city, the Information Minister reported that coalition forces "are not near Baghdad. . . . They are not even [within] 100 miles."

The same response to bad news happens in our workplaces daily: Denial, deception, embarrassment, and fear lead to delay in telling bad news—even when the consequences threaten to engulf people.

Here's a bad-news situation that puzzled people for years, according to the former vice president of engineering at a large oil company:

"We had an oil well that didn't fit any correlations. Then as we drilled other wells nearby, this particular well still didn't correlate. The well had wandered off a half mile from surface location. The company had fal-

I don't want any yes-men around me. I want everyone to tell me the truth—even though it costs him his job.
—Samuel Goldwyn

sified records during the drilling to hide the fact that they were drilling behind the specified contract deviation—27° deviation from vertical. That's why no one could figure it out for 15 years and why it cost us so much money through the years to drill extra wells to study the situation. Somebody made a mistake, and nobody wanted to give the bad news."

Often, the shoe is on the leader's foot. If the news is a layoff, the executive may not want to disappoint or anger others. So he or she says as little as possible, as late as possible.

According to a recent study done by The International Association of Business Communicators, only 37 percent of companies actually use face-to-face meetings to deliver bad news. Their typical modus operandi? E-mail and letters carry the bad news most often—40 percent of the time. (See Figure 2.1.)

Some justify the method as efficient and fast. Others aren't so kind about the motive for the method.

Figure 2.1
"I Have Bad News—Sit Down"

E-mail	28%
Face-to-face meetings with supervisors	19%
Face-to-face meetings with senior leaders	18%
Formal letter/memo from executives	12%
Employee Web site	8%
Tele- or videoconference	6%
Newsletter	4%

Only 37 percent of organizations give bad news face to face.
Source: International Association of Business Communicators

The Risk of Broken Limbs or Promises

Good news can also be a problem. Some people fear providing information because the details involve risk. They fear making promises, setting up false expectations, or being held accountable for results. If you say, "We're tracking along at a 28 percent growth rate" and there's a dip later, people are going to ask why. If you say you're going to cut expenses by 15 percent and you can't, you're going to have to explain what you tried that didn't work. If you say you're going to investigate ways to improve the traffic congestion around the building, they'll expect you to do it.

People figure that no promises are better than broken promises, so they don't go out on a limb with any kind of prediction, commitment, or goal that they'll need to meet.

The "I Hear You, I Hear You, I Hear You" Syndrome

Let's face it. Some people give incomplete information because they just don't listen to questions others ask and don't pay attention to what others tell them. We're preoccupied, pressed for time, and busy prioritizing our own plans. Conversations chug along like this one I had a few days ago with an account manager:

Me: Is the client going to cancel Jacque's program because of the hurricane?

Manager: That program was last week. It's over.

Me: If they're canceling, did they agree to cover the airfare? It was a nonrefundable ticket.

So much for listening. Guilty as charged. Some people lack the skill to think on their feet. When caught off guard in the hallway or in a meeting, they rant and ramble without supplying a complete, coherent, succinct response to a question or statement of their opinion on an issue. They never stop, listen, and think before they speak.

Despite What Your Momma May Say, Tell All You Know

A change in direction can be one of the most critical things people need to know. Yet according to the results of a study of 1,845 U.S. workers, conducted in September 2006 by Hudson, a New York staffing and outsourcing firm, half of the workforce reported that they rarely, if ever, receive information from their managers about strategic or organizational changes. The leader makes a U-turn. And nobody tells the rest of the crew. Big problem.

So how do you keep people from doubting your intentions when they're not hearing all you know? Perception forms immediately. You're either open or tight-lipped with information. What's the antidote to confusion, at best, and distrust, at the worst?

Explain Your Reasoning behind Decisions

People may not agree with your decisions and actions, but at least they'll be glad to know what they are. What are the facts? What are the criteria? What are the extenuating circumstances? What other suppliers' and partners' actions affect the decisions and deadlines? What are the wild cards that no one controls? What are the certainties and what are your guesstimates? What complexities can foul things up at the last moment? Without such information, your decisions and actions sound arbitrary. Rationale, however right or wrong, provides a sense of fairness and justice. Without the details, people rarely buy into the mission for the long haul.

Focus on the How, Not Just the What

Unless you're running for the Oval Office, tell people how you plan to implement things. Mushroom management whereby everyone is kept in the dark about *how* you're going to provide "value-added service" or "a unique customer experience," or "bring innovative products to market" no longer works.

But specificity in stating goals is not the only "how" that needs to be spelled out.

When you praise someone, focus on the how—how they got the good rating. Otherwise, how will they know what to repeat?

In statements of values or ethics, once again, communicate the how. How will people recognize good ethics or your values when they see them? You say you value risk. How do they evaluate risk in your department? What's acceptable risk? What's an act of lunacy? You say you reward commitment. How will you measure that?

Be Relevant Rather Than Resented

Go home and announce something as specific and personal as a job change, and see if family members don't sift the details differently. Your spouse asks how much raise goes with the increased job responsibilities. Your teens want to know if they have to change schools. Your in-laws want to know if you're moving the grandkids across the country. Your CPA tells you whether you're better or worse off after the tax hit. The same information or "news" means different things to different people. Don't expect your different audiences to do your work for you.

Interpret information and translate the relevant details to the different people or groups involved. Think about what your information means to them specifically and clarify that when you share your news.

Mention the Measures You're Tracking

Whatever you measure, share it. Let's talk financials for a moment. If yours is a public company, the numbers get reported anyway. If it's a private company, somebody has to do the calculations and that person will be tempted to talk to friends and coworkers. When the real numbers don't add up to the stated explanations, trust plummets.

Numbers held close to the vest typically are used to justify "no's." No raises. No bonuses. No creature comforts. No building improvements. No pet projects.

Ditto for other measures—goals, calls taken per hour, leads generated, sales closed, markets opened, widgets rejected, data researched. Whatever numbers you measure, mention them.

Designate a Go-To Person for
Follow-Up Details or Questions

Okay, so you're busy and don't have time to answer daily e-mails and phone calls from 60,000 employees, 3,700 customers, 420 suppliers, and 19 strategic partners. Somebody else does. Tag that somebody as the go-to person for follow-up information on key concerns or issues—especially after major announcements, a change in policy, or a new procedure.

Don't Hide behind the Technology

No doubt you could still function as a relatively normal human being yet never speak to another person on this planet. You can order food, pay your utilities, do your banking, buy birthday gifts, and contact your representatives in Congress online. I don't recommend it as a way of life, however.

> *Pick up the phone or walk down the hall to the next cubicle occasionally.*

Neither do I recommend it in the workplace. What takes 10 e-mails to negotiate or clarify can often be communicated in a three-minute phone conversation. Pick up the phone or walk down the hall to the next cubicle occasionally.

Tell Bad News Promptly: Never Underestimate the Importance of the Two-Minute Warning

Without the two-minute warning in a ball game, the trailing team may miss their chance to redouble their efforts to catch up before the final buzzer sounds. The game ends; they lose. Ditto for communicating in business. The worse the news, the sooner people need to know it and the more effort should go into communicating it.

A director of operations at a client organization remembers problems associated with the move-in to their design research center. "When we design a new center, we always need a wide variety of compressed gases such as nitrogen, helium, and so forth in the lab. We had a guy responsible for the seven processes, all of which need these gases. About two months away from occupancy, I checked the drawings for that suite and didn't notice the specialty gases on the plans. I thought there was an error in the drawings. So I call him in and I ask, 'Are you aware there're no specialty gases in that lab?' "

" 'Yes,' he says, rather matter-of-factly. He'd known it for five months! But he was going to wait until we got ready to move in and say, 'Hey, there's a problem. We can't move in—I just noticed there are no gases in here.' He was afraid somebody would be upset with him! If we'd known about the problem five months earlier, we could have started getting the gases in there at that point. As it was, we were two months from scheduled move-in already, and getting the gases in there would take us at least another three months. All because he was afraid to tell somebody!"

If giving bad news gives you the shakes . . .

. . . Focus on the next step: If some action or inaction on your part has caused the problem, explain what steps you've taken to date to correct the situation and what options you think may be appropriate as next steps. In other words, instead of dumping the problem, assume the position of "I'm advising you of a major problem. Here's what I'm thinking and doing about it, and I need your input to go further."

. . . Share your ego strength: Shoulder any responsibility that's yours. Assume that others may take out their anger on you, the message bearer; that's human nature. Then try to focus their attention on the problem or issue and the solution.

Bad news is bad news—whether it's going up the chain,

down the chain, or laterally in an organization. With the two-minute warning, you have a chance to mitigate the damage. With no warning, the consequences can be severe.

Frame Negative News Positively
When You Can Do So Honestly

"Inside every cloud there's a silver lining" became a cliché for good reason. However, its truth should not be tossed aside without due consideration in bad-news situations. If your team sees the glass as half empty, you have every right—even obligation—to help them see it as half full.

Instead of hiding the complete details, provide them in such a compelling way that you gain buy-in for your action plan. Case in point from a seasoned CEO who announced a salary freeze to his ailing organization in the high-tech industry shortly after he took the helm: After crunching the numbers, he became increasingly aware that his predecessor had approved annual raises and bonuses at the expense of capital improvements, research and development, and marketing efforts. As a result, the competition had outstripped them, and they lagged far behind in the industry. Armed with industry charts of compensation studies, competitor pricing, R&D budgeting for prior years, capital budgets and projects put on hold, he laid out the facts to his employees. Then he summed up this way:

"In almost all job classifications, according to industry averages, you're overpaid. The good news: We're not going to lower your salary. The bad news: We'll not be giving any more cost-of-living raises for the next three years. Any bonuses will be based on performance and contribution. We can't afford to do otherwise or none of us will have jobs five years from now. Take a look at the facts. Punch holes in the information I've given you if you can.

Let's talk about the reasoning behind this decision. I'm open for questions."

They asked. But with complete information that had been missing in previous years and a straightforward explanation about the future, the CEO gained their trust and buy-in. Today, the glass is three-quarters full.

Negative news is no time for withholding. It's time for prompt truth telling in a positive frame of mind with a clear plan of action.

Develop More than a "We've Always Been Lucky" Crisis Plan

Listen to those on-the-street interviews after a crisis strikes—natural disaster, power outage in the state, terrorist attack, computer hacker stealing all the company's trade secrets. The reporter asks the vice president, "So do you have a back-up plan to get the situation back to normal?"

"Well, up until now we've just always been lucky, I guess . . ." and he or she begins to explain the company's lack of a back-up plan. "We just never thought something like this would happen here."

It might happen here. There. At your place. Whatever the "it" might be. So *before* a crisis strikes, have a crisis plan and communicate the details to everyone who needs to know.

I'm not necessarily talking about your single-handed responsibility to shut down Manhattan. I'm talking about your plan to reproduce documents when the power goes off in the building and you have reports and proposals due to clients. I'm not talking about landing the plane in Iran in case of a terrorist attack. I'm talking about landing the client project in case the competition offers a 20 percent discount to close the deal. I'm not talking about when the water supply in Los Angeles gets poisoned. I'm talking about when your building gets flooded and employees need to get their work done.

Crises happen weekly: The deaths of several senior executives in a private plane crash. The resignation of a key employee. The bankruptcy of a primary supplier. A tornado ripping through the center of downtown. When it's a major crisis, consider these key steps:

▶ Remember that "no news" is news. Have a voice mailbox for employees to monitor status for updates, even when the updates say "nothing has changed."

▶ Tell what you're investigating or considering—even if you have discovered no causes or resolutions. ("Here's what we're investigating. . . ." "The facts that we've discovered to date are these . . ." "The situation is changing rapidly. What we think we may do now is . . . But that may change within the next eight hours. . . .")

▶ Ask for people's patience. Patience is common sense, but that gets trampled in emergencies.

▶ Keep suppliers and partners up to date so they're part of the solution, not part of the problem.

▶ Communicate the backup plans and logistics before needing them.

▶ When the crisis is minor or routine, be thankful.

Communicate Like You Brush Your Teeth

Make it a habit. Do it frequently, habitually, systematically. Get a system, a channel, a structure, a timetable that works for you. Informal chats in the hallway. Fireside chats in the lobby. Factory visits by the big-cheese. Morning meetings between shifts. One-on-one meetings with each team lead. Message boards in the restrooms. Weekly teleconferencing or videoconferencing. Monthly skip meetings. Company or department newsletters. Paycheck stuffers. E-mail blasts before or after lunch. Chat sessions on the intranet. Hotlines for questions. Blogs by your brother-in-law. Voicemail solos with your sister. Just do it regularly.

Never Fear to Be Fallible

Leaders sometimes feel that they can instill confidence in others by comments like these: "We're on top of the situation." "Everything's under control." "Don't worry. We're on it. It's being handled."

But trust and commitment rise when others feel they are included in the situation. And should the previous claims prove untrue, trust plummets. Consider communicating openly with language that implies you may just be fallible:

► "We're aware of the situation—we're monitoring it."

► "The situation's on our radar—we're watching it closely."

► "In this situation, here's what I think is the best way to go and why. . . ."

► "Here's my position on the issue and what my data says. . . ."

> *When you have to eat crow on occasion, it goes down much easier when mixed with a dash of humility and a pinch of honesty. Plus, people don't consider it so much fun to watch you choke.*

- ▶ "The deciding factor in a situation such as this has to be. . . ."
- ▶ "Here's what I'm going to be recommending to my boss and why. . . ."
- ▶ "We considered three alternative approaches. I want to explain them, and I think you'll see why we chose the first option. . . ."

When you have to eat crow on occasion, it goes down much easier when mixed with a dash of humility and a pinch of honesty. Plus, people don't consider it so much fun to watch you choke.

CHAPTER 3

Is It Clear?

*A great many people think that
polysyllables are a sign of intelligence.*
—BARBARA WALTERS

Y ou can't just go anywhere at any time you like," the warden at the federal prison in Yuma, Arizona, explained to the soon-to-be parolee. "You're going to be wearing an ankle sensor to allow the parole officer to monitor your whereabouts. You'll be allowed to leave your house between 7 a.m. and 6 p.m. for work. But other than that, you'll have only a small window of opportunity to leave your house. Do you understand?"

"Yeah. Just which window should I use?" the convict asked.

Conversations around your conference table sometimes may not be much clearer than this miscommunication the prison warden shared with me after a keynote in his city. Both written and spoken snafus surface everywhere. The difference between safe operations and tragedy may hinge on a garbled statement, a single misused word, an unstated assumption, an invalid conclusion, a euphemism, or a nonverbal cue that nixes the verbal.

We all *think* we're clear communicators; otherwise, we wouldn't say what we do. So what signals trouble, and which safeguards ensure success?

Beware the Blank Stare

At my "Get Your Book Published" workshop, I was leading attendees to formulate their book idea for a proposal to a literary agent. It was Susan's turn to "pitch" her book concept to the group. After her pitch, the group fell totally silent—not a word of feedback from anyone. Finally, someone spoke up, "I don't get it—could you elaborate?" She gladly did so for the next five minutes. Gradually, the group "got" her concept—and gave her intriguing feedback for the next 10 minutes.

But then the strangest thing happened. During the remainder of the seminar, Susan never changed the way she worded her pitch letter—even after it met with that first collective blank stare. It didn't seem to occur to her that her original pitch lacked clarity—that if nobody "got it," she should change the way she expressed the written pitch.

The same thing happens back on the job. The boss drafts a report and asks a staff member to proofread it. The assistant brings the report back with a section marked and says, "I don't understand what you mean here," To which the boss replies, "Oh, that's technical—it'll be clear to the lawyers when they review it." Two weeks later, the lawyers ask for a rewrite of the same section.

I've watched this scene unfold time and time again. People always assume the confusion happens on the other end of the communication—that what they themselves say is perfectly clear and that the *other* person just missed it somehow. A better gauge of our own clarity: Beware the blank stare.

If you need additional signs that you're not getting through, consider these:

- ▶ *Lack of questions.* (You call for questions at the end of a presentation, and there are none. Or, you bring up an idea in a meeting and you're greeted with only polite smiles.)
- ▶ *Unexpected responses.* (People respond irrationally to what you say, such as with anger, withdrawal, silence, or denial.)
- ▶ *Lack of coordination.* (Things "fall between the cracks" in coordinating projects.)
- ▶ *Rework.* (Projects have to be redone because the instructions weren't clear the first time. Or, extra work was completed "just in case" to "cover all the bases" because somebody wasn't sure what was needed.)
- ▶ *Low morale.* (People feel discouraged that they can never "get it right" when, in fact, projects are frequently delegated without essential elements for successful completion.)

We need objective measures of clarity. That's why organizations pay pollsters to take their temperature periodically—to let their leaders know how well they're communicating.

Results from the latest Communication Effectiveness Consortium, brought together by Towers Perrin, a global professional services firm, suggest that 63 percent of employees say their senior leaders effectively communicate their goals.

That means 37 percent still do not. And we're talking about the senior leaders here—those who have access to assistants and the finest technology to help them shape and deliver the message. Those managers and supervisors lower in the organization have even less help in shaping their messages—yet their communication with their direct reports is what matters most in the day-to-day operations.

And if you're a leader of a project team, a committee, or other group without an official title, you have even less access to assistants, consultants, technology, and budget to get your message out. But as a leader and go-to person who shapes opinions of those around you, your communication becomes critical to daily success.

Everybody has to measure how clearly he or she communicates. The most basic question to ask: Do people "get it"? Do they understand the goal—the what, the why, and the how?

What a Hoot When People Convolute

Clear messages start with clear words. Clear words lead to clear action. Fuzzy words result in fuzzy action or no action.

Here are a couple of excerpts from documents gathered through the years—written by otherwise well-educated people:

> "The efficiency with which an operation utilizes its available equipment is an influential factor in productivity."
>
> **Translation:** "If you use your equipment efficiently, you can do more."

Not exactly a profound concept.

> "The current Division B headcount exceeds the requirements to support the current revenue level and

results in a 15 percent decrease in revenue per direct headcount year-over-year. However, most of this headcount is being utilized to cover unplanned vacation and training requirements. This increased utilization of excess direct manpower on indirect activities appears to be the primary factor for the declining margin performance against plan. We should note that there are other operational issues such as exempt time reporting, partially utilized headcount at remote sites, accounting issues, and bid margin projections, which need to be addressed. Please be advised that unless project revenue increases, any incremental labor costs will increase period costs and further reduce margins."

Translation: "Our profit margin on the Division B project has dropped by 15 percent this quarter because of increased labor costs. Several operational issues, however, cause us to doubt the accuracy of that figure: exempt-time reporting, staffing at remote sites, accounting procedures, and the accuracy of our original projections."

Here's another example you may have seen from your bank or credit card company:

"Rolling consecutive twelve-month billing cycle period."

Translation: "The next 12 months."

Why do people muddle simple messages? There are several reasons.

A False Sense of "Professionalism" and Formality

Here are excerpts from two cover letters we recently received for an accounting position in our organization:

First Applicant: "From the specifications listed in your advertisement, my varied experience covers a wide range of skills and responsibilities in which I have been very successful across several functional areas in multiple industries. If what you seek is a conscientious, determined collaborator, then do consider an interview where I may convey my interest and suitability with your organization."

Second Applicant: "I'm a self-employed CPA, working for clients in small to midsize organizations. I think my varied industry experience would be an asset in the accounting responsibilities you described in the *Dallas Morning News*. May I discuss this opening with you in person?"

Having run a consulting firm for the past 26 years, I've discovered in our presentations and writing workshops that some people consider themselves more "professional" if they string together long sentences and big words. My response: More professional to whom? Not to any professional writers or speakers I know.

Bad Models

When bosses delegate projects (documents, presentations, speeches), the typical thing—and often the first thing—people do is to search for a model. Bad models exist everywhere. Just because you hear someone else spewing out garbage doesn't mean that the message was clear the first time, that the format was easy to follow, that the document got action, or that the argument changed minds.

Elevating the Importance of What They Do

People use jargon to create meaning out of the mundane in the same way cooks use steak sauce to flavor a tough T-bone. Nurses no longer make rounds and "give out medicine," but rather "dispense medications." Instead of police "pulling suspects from their cars," they now "extract them from their vehicles." The Information Technology (IT) expert can either "burn an extra copy of a DVD" or "use a peripheral drive to create a set of redundant files stored on a digital video disc." Your Web master may tell you either that the text on the Web page has been changed or that "the HTML source codes were manipulated to display an alternate message in the browser."

> *People use jargon to create meaning out of the mundane in the same way cooks use steak sauce to flavor a tough T-bone.*

In fact, the whole jargon routine at work reminds me of a scene in *Batman Returns*. After Batman (Bruce Wayne in costume) is exposed to poisonous gas, a friend named Mr. Fox—a scientist from Wayne Enterprises—comes to his aid.

Mr. Fox: I analyzed your blood, isolating the receptor compounds in the protein-based catalyst.
Bruce Wayne: Am I meant to understand any of that?

Mr. Fox: Not at all. I just wanted you to know how *hard* it was.

For the most part, even when people want to know "how hard it was," they prefer that you tell them in plain English.

Phoniness/Insincerity

If you're inviting me to your wedding, I expect to read: "Mr. and Mrs. Dominique Patel request the honor of your presence at the marriage of their daughter, Christy Leigh, to Mr. Perry Tubaine, on the 9th of September at four o'clock in the afternoon."

> *People will frighten you about a graduation. They use words you don't hear often. "And we wish you Godspeed." It is a warning, Godspeed. It means you are no longer welcome here at these prices.*
>
> —BILL COSBY

But I don't expect to read such syntax and formality in an e-mail inviting me to the departmental planning meeting where we'll discuss "strategic initiatives designed to enhance our capabilities to respond to opportunities afforded us to increase visibility both within the parameters of assigned roles and outside the targeted functional areas of future growth." Such language rings false.

Ignorance on a Subject

If you don't know what you're talking about but can say it with enough buzzwords, maybe nobody will be able to follow your explanation long enough to ask any questions. A client in the IT department of an energy company explains this as the key discriminator in hiring outside contractors to write software documentation for them. "If we ask them to come in and learn an in-house program and they can write a page or two of documentation in plain English, we figure they understand the program pretty well. But if we ask them to write us a page or two of sample documentation, and they send us something filled with jargon, we know they don't have a clue what they're talking about."

Intimidation

Have you ever called a lawyer to ask a technical question and had him or her beat you up with the answer? That is, the lawyer rattles off an answer as if lecturing a group of graduate students ready to take the bar exam? Did you ask a second question? Many people don't—and that's the idea behind the use of jargon as a tool for intimidation. The game goes like this: "When I can't out-reason you, I can out-buzz you, so you don't understand what the heck I said."

> *Have you ever noticed that the smaller the idea, the bigger the words used to express it?*
>
> —ANONYMOUS

Use Plain English

If a phrase starts to roll off your tongue, shut your mouth; consider it a cliché—probably a phrase so overused that the meaning has long since been lost. Instead, aim for originality and specificity. For starters, here's a list of bureaucratic buzzwords that muddy messages and mar your image as a clear communicator and straight shooter:

▶ *No-brainer* (meaning if you don't see it as clearly as I do, you're off your rocker)

▶ *Enhancement* (an improvement too insignificant to charge for but worth touting; often confused with body parts)

▶ *Value-added* (anything you can't charge for because the client doesn't value it enough to pay for it)

▶ *Value-proposition* (proposing differing shtick to see what flies)

▶ *Incent* (prodding people with money, freebies, coupons—whatever it takes to get them to do something they're not inclined to do on their own)

▶ *Core competencies* (as opposed to core incompetencies?)

▶ *Initiatives* (long, long ago, these were called goals and plans)

▶ *Thought leaders* (as opposed to those who lead the unthinking morons?)

▶ *Optimization* (the process of making things better and better—as in cooking, flying, making love, making stealth missiles, making movies, building skyscrapers, counting votes, applying makeup, charting sea turtles)

▶ *Solution* (solid dissolved in a liquid or a mathematical proof hidden inside all products and services now offered by all corporations around the world)

▶ *Alignment* (identifying where the rubber doesn't meet the road in goals that are supposed to be running parallel to yours)

▶ *Deliverables* (paperboys and girls used to ride bikes and carry these)

- *Rightsizing* (Nordstrom does this free of charge if the clothes are pricey enough)
- *Moral clarity* (when you decide you can't get away with something without being fined or jailed)
- *Impactful* (newly coined term meaning packed full of potential to be hard-hitting—in the mind, heart, pocketbook, gut, mouth)
- *Robust* (fat, wealthy, expensive, complex, healthy, meaningful, deep, feisty; can be applied to people, philosophy, technology, equipment, training, strategy, food, religion, research, vegetation, medicine, light bulbs, laughter, beer)
- *Branding* (marking livestock so it doesn't get lost or stolen; marking dead stock in inventory that hasn't sold in years with a new "look and feel" so that it finds its way to market again)
- *Methodologies* (in more primitive times, this was *methods* or the way you do something)
- *Technologies* (yet undiscovered wizardry from the netherworld)
- *Bandwidth* (refers to anything you want to limit, as in "that's outside our bandwidth")
- *Seamless* (meaning, I don't know where the heck my job ends and yours starts, so we can pass the buck if necessary)
- *Platform* (horizontal structure that supports all systems, people, brands, and philosophies)

Stringing these terms together in paragraph after paragraph from document to document makes communication bland and meaningless. Take a look at this excerpt from an annual report of a Fortune 10 company to see if you find anything thought provoking:

> Our industry is constantly evolving. The industry has globalized as the world's economies have expanded. Partners and competition change. New opportunities are larger, more capital intensive, and often in remote areas or difficult physical environments. Business cycles fluctuate, but our long-term view provides us with consistent direction. Finally, technology has improved the methods we employ and the results we achieve in meeting the world's energy challenges.

Any great revelation here? Nothing specific. Could have come from any energy company in the market—or remove the word *energy* and you could insert it in just about any annual report. Bureaucratic. Bland. Boring. What in the world are they doing behind closed doors? Paragraphs like this make shareholders wonder, where in the world is Waldo working?

Bureaucratic. Bland. Boring. What in the world are they doing behind closed doors? Paragraphs like this make shareholders wonder, where in the world is Waldo working?

Start with the Punch Line

Mike Duffy, a former senior manager working for a subsidiary of Occidental Petroleum, learned this principle the hard way. During the transition period after his company was acquired, his team had been experiencing delays in getting their budgets approved for special projects. One specific pipeline repair presented what his engineering team considered a grave danger. The vice president of operations of the acquired division wrote memo after memo over a six-month period, asking for budget approval on money to repair the pipeline. No response from headquarters.

The situation reached a critical point. During this interim period one Friday, I was in Mike's organization working on another project. He mentioned his concern and asked me to take a look at his document requesting the budget approval to repair the pipeline. The problem was immediately apparent. His punch line—his request for approval for the money to repair the dangerous pipeline—was literally in the last paragraph of the two-page document. I suggested that he reverse the structure.

On Tuesday, Mike had his money—along with this note from the legendary Armand Hammer, then CEO of Occidental: "Why haven't I been notified of this problem before now?" The documents had repeatedly landed on his desk apparently unread because the bottom-line message remained buried.

People may argue that others won't understand the message without a little background information. But actually the opposite is true: People will never understand the background until they know your point.

You are reminded of this principle every time you listen to a voice mail that sounds like an autobiography before somebody gets around to stating their purpose and phone number.

> *People may argue that others won't understand the message without a little background information. But actually the opposite is true: People will never understand the background until they know your point.*

Granted, there are exceptions: Movies, TV sitcoms, and jokes. Before the network takes you to commercial, the teaser plunges you into the middle of the action. Then for the next half hour, you wind your way out of the dilemma. But for those information sessions where amusement is not the primary focus, start with the punch line.

Whether delivering a presentation, writing an e-mail, or briefing somebody in the hallway, make the opening line the punch line.

Specifics—or Just Semantics?

How many times have you heard this comment interjected in a heated discussion: "Well, I think it's just a matter of semantics." Of course it is! Words mean something. And therein lies the problem. For example, take the controversy swirling around the issue of illegal immigration in our country. One politician refers to the "amnesty" issue and outlines a plan whereby a person already in the country illegally can earn legal status. Another politician contradicts the first politician's concept and plan altogether by saying that *amnesty* means "forgiveness"; therefore, any plan to "earn" citizenship isn't an amnesty plan at all. The amnesty dialogue is but one example of the point.

Words have meanings, and those meanings are not just a simple matter of semantics. Brushing them aside with "I think we're really saying the same thing; it's just a matter of semantics," creates a dangerous intersection if people intend to arrive at agreement somewhere down the road.

> *Words carry the crux of conversation. Selection is central to understanding and agreement.*

Words carry the crux of

conversation. Selection is central to understanding and agreement.

In fact, many customer complaints can be traced to this one root cause—a vague word with a different meaning to service agent and customer. The salesperson says, "We should be able to work out a substantial discount if you want to take the floor model." (The salesperson has in mind a 20 percent discount; the customer is thinking a 50 percent discount.) The supplier says, "We'll call you in a few days when the shipment comes in." (The supplier is thinking two to three weeks; the customer is thinking two to three days.)

Neither do we fare much better with specific, precise internal communication.

For example, you ask another department to help you with a project, and they respond that they'll be unable to do so because of *limited resources*. Are they talking about money, time, equipment, or expertise?

The HR department tells you they've had a *number of calls* from employees upset about the policy just announced. How many calls? 7? 17? 70? 700?

The vice president of marketing tells you that the company has had *a significant increase* in the number of leads generated by a new marketing campaign. What kind of increase comes to mind? 12 percent? 20 percent? 40 percent?

A client promises to call you back *within a few days* with an answer about whether she intends to renew a multimillion-dollar contract with your organization. When do you expect an answer? Three days? A week? Two weeks? Would it matter which client said this to you?

A strategic partner suggests that you take advantage of some of their *promotional activities* as you jointly introduce your services to a new industry. Is the partner talking about attending trade shows? Sharing the cost for direct mail?

Hosting a hospitality suite at their next conference? Sponsoring their speaker at your next event? Putting reciprocating links or banner ads on your Web sites?

You may have had the tree swing experience in your own organization (see Figure 3.1). The situation would be funny if it didn't happen so frequently.

When semantics enters the conversation, the conversation is no longer about semantics. Choose the precise word. Nail down the specifics.

Avoid the Template Tease

Templates save time and ensure consistency. But like a tailor's tacking on the hem of your pants, a template serves as the starting point, not the finished product.

Organizations have tried to turn everything into a template: training, e-mail responses to customers, Help Desk responses, sales presentations, cafeteria menus, conference and trade show agendas.

> *Templates save time and ensure consistency. But like a tailor's tacking on the hem of your pants, a template serves as the starting point, not the finished product.*

Here's the conversation I had last week when I called my cable company and finally got through to their Help Desk:

"How may I help you?"

"My Internet connection is down. I understand there's some problem in the neighborhood. Just as I pulled into my driveway tonight, your cable van was sitting in front of my house, and two service people were standing outside on my lawn. They said they were waiting on a callback

Figure 3.1

The Tree Swing Experience Happens Too Frequently to Be Funny

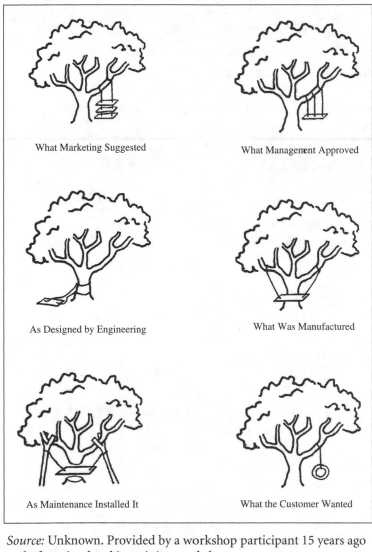

What Marketing Suggested

What Management Approved

As Designed by Engineering

What Was Manufactured

As Maintenance Installed It

What the Customer Wanted

Source: Unknown. Provided by a workshop participant 15 years ago and often circulated in training workshops.

from their supervisor to see if he was going to give approval to replace the lines out here tonight or if they were going to wait until tomorrow. I wanted to know what the status is."

"Okay, let me check." Silence. He comes back on the line. "No, everything's working fine here. Your computer should be working fine."

"Sir, maybe you didn't hear me. My Internet connection is completely down. I have no service at all. Your cable truck is parked down the street now, and the two servicemen say there's trouble with the lines in the neighborhood."

"We have no report of that. Let's do a step-by-step check. First, would you check the lights on your modem and tell me if the top light is blinking green?"

"Sir, NO lights are blinking. There seems to be an outage in the whole neighborhood."

"I have no report of that."

"I am telling you that now. Your cable truck is parked outside my house, and that's what your service agents just told me. There is trouble in the neighborhood, and I'm asking if you will check with a service supervisor to see when they intend to install a new line—tonight, tomorrow, or later this week."

"Would you just look at the modem and tell me if the top light is blinking green?"

"Sir, the top light is NOT blinking. I have NO connection at all. Cable service is down in our neighborhood. Your service people are working about 200 yards from my house. They say they are waiting for approval to install a new line. I just want to know if the line will be installed *tonight* so I can get some work done here."

"From here, it seems that your connection is working properly. Let's do a step-by-step check, please. Would you look at your modem and tell me if the green light or any light is blinking?"

At this point I realize I'm caught in a loop, talking to a person tied to a procedural template. I hang up with the "Help Desk" and walk outside to find the repair guys, who've now pulled their truck further down the street.

Written templates, just like procedural templates, tease customers and employees alike, making people think they might get a real answer to their questions.

Here's another nightmare—a form letter mailed in response to a customer request to switch their membership from Plan Option A to Plan Option B on a particular legal services policy. Instead of switching the policy and changing their billing information accordingly, the customer repeatedly received this form letter rather than the corrective action.

Dear Member:

Your membership will no longer be available through payroll deduction. We value your continued membership and want to make the necessary transition as easy as possible. Your membership is as important to us as it is to you. To avoid the loss of your valuable benefits, just select the payment method most convenient for you so that you may continue to receive uninterrupted services. If you have questions regarding this form or your membership, please contact the Customer Care Department at 1-800-XXX-XXXX.

Each time the customer called to ask why headquarters wasn't switching the membership from Option A to Option B and changing the invoicing procedure appropriately, she continued to receive this same form letter—with no answers. It took several phone calls from the customer

and from the legal services provider's own salesperson—
and a formal customer letter to headquarters to stop this
unhelpful template and get an answer to the billing question.

Such template responses tempt employees to jump from
the twelfth floor and cause customers to pay 50 percent
more to buy from the competition.

Provide Context—Even in Jell-O

Providing context for a comment can mean the difference
between a performance bonus and a prison sentence. For
example, an executive at Universal Inc. states to investors
at the annual shareholders meeting that orders are back-
logged and profits are lagging behind expectations. If the
executive makes that same comment at breakfast with only
the fund manager and analyst present, that's grounds for
charges of insider trading.

The scandal involving former congressman Mark Foley
and his sexually explicit messages written to teenage pages
working in Congress basically turns on an issue of context.
Were the messages written *while* the pages were in the in-
tern program or only *after* they left the program? Context—Were the e-mails sent from someone in a position
of power over the teens?—may mean the difference in legal rulings.

After the bombing of the Federal Building in Oklahoma
City, the civilians in charge of the cleanup sent word to the
Federal Emergency Management Agency (FEMA) that
they needed "decontamination units." What the re-
questors had in mind were shower units to hose down
workers as they came off the heaps of rubble. What the
FEMA officers began searching for were nuclear deconta-

mination units—the meaning of the request in their typical context.

Osama Bin Laden continues to release tapes saying that the United States brought all the terrorist attacks upon itself by its own actions. Yet parts of the released tapes showing the terrorists' plans for the attacks were completed at a time when things in the Middle East were going well—just after all parties had signed the Middle East Peace Accord. So the very context of Osama Bin Laden's words makes them untrue.

Establishing context becomes even more difficult when the framework resembles Jell-O—that is, when the context remains fluid and flexible over a long period of time, such as during a merger or during a long product-development cycle. But difficult or not, context provides both the clues and the flavor of the message.

Assume at Your Own Risk

The previous year had not been a good one financially. While revenues had grown, our profits lagged. Primarily, the problem centered around new sales staff coming on board who had not met quota. Despite team training, one-on-one coaching, and administrative support, the situation with one key salesperson had not improved. As the cliché goes, I wanted to "light a fire under him" in one more attempt to let him know how urgent it was that the company see some return on our investment.

So in an all-hands "state of the company" meeting, I laid out the financial picture, set financial goals for the coming year, and outlined key initiatives necessary to achieve these goals. As a wrap-up, I mentioned the total cost and overhead each sales rep was responsible for before he or she was at a breakeven point to "cover" him- or herself. I ended with the total figure that we'd invested over the past three years in bringing on new reps and the individual deficit when reps did not meet quota.

When I finished with the financial picture, I paused for feedback. The nonperforming sales rep commented with all sincerity: "I feel really valued—that you'd invest this much in us and that you believe in us this strongly."

Verification can be vital. The point I thought I had made so very clearly was not the conclusion the recipient drew from the discussion. It's not an uncommon problem. Talking with a vice president of another organization recently, I heard a similar tale.

> We have had six regional directors gathered around the conference table every month for the last six months looking at the same numbers. And every month, we discuss the numbers, saying, "This number has to change." The number in question was in Weldon's region. He would nod and agree, but he did nothing. Next month, same thing. We'd all six sit around the table and look at the reports and say, "This number has to change." Weldon would nod and agree. Next month, same thing. Same number. I didn't think he was getting it. So I sent someone out to talk to him one-on-one and deliver the message—that he had to improve that number. Basically, it was one single problem he had to take care of in his region. Six months later, he still hadn't done anything to correct the situation.
>
> So come December, the last two weeks of the year, when he should have been putting in an all-out effort on the problem, he decided to take a two-week vaca-

tion. I finally had to terminate him. I've never seen anyone so shocked. Total shock. Yet, for six months, we all looked at the numbers, and we all clearly agreed that those numbers in his department had to change. I don't know what he concluded after each of those six meetings. But evidently, the message wasn't clear—that *he* had to do something to correct the problem in his region.

As long as communication goes only one way, we tend to assume that people walk away from a conversation with the point we thought we made very clearly. Yet that's a frequent complaint about nonproductive meetings: Attendees walk out mumbling, "So what was decided? Are we or are we not going to X . . . ?" Only the subject changes.

> *Anyone who isn't confused here doesn't really understand what's going on.*
> —NIGEL WRENCH

To make sure people walk away with the same message you intended to convey, verify by getting them to react to it in some fashion. These statements might be helpful to verify that they heard what you intended: "How do you think this policy will affect your staff?" "What objections do you think people in your area might have?" "What are some of the first steps you'd suggest to make this change reality?" "How easy (or hard) do you think this will be?" "What questions do you think we'll hear in the first 90 days as we roll out this program?"

Questions like these generate the comments that verify people really do understand your point. From there, you know whether to circle back or head home.

Make Sure Your Nonverbal Cues
Don't Contradict Your Words

Tell a nonperformer that her behavior is unacceptable, but smile and nod encouragement at the wrong time during your discussion, and she may walk out thinking "no big deal" and revert to the status quo. Announce to the media that the customer reports about defects in your product are isolated incidents—but do it with a furrowed brow and you may have lawyers soliciting class-action claims by noon. Tell your team that "things are under control" and that you have the boss's complete confidence. But do it with a nervous fidget and they may wonder if you'll hold your job long enough to report the team's recommendations at all.

> *Words alone never carry the complete message. Messages come from context, relationship, timing, tone of voice, what was said, what was not said, and body language. All these things together comprise the total message that people "hear."*

Words alone never carry the complete message. Messages come from context, relationship, timing, tone of voice, what was said, what was not said, and body language. All these things together comprise the total message that people "hear."

Adapt Your Style to the Person and Purpose

George S. Patton, more affectionately known as "Old Blood and Guts," graduated from West Point in 1909 and was commissioned as an officer in the U.S. Army. From a wealthy and educated family, he was introduced to

Homer's *Iliad* and *Odyssey*, the *Bible*, and Shakespeare from an early age. Classical literature and military history remained an interest of his throughout his lifetime.

Yet when he spoke to the troops on the frontlines, he spoke their language. He used no metaphors from mythology. His purpose was action, not theory. The lower ranking the group, the more tactical his message.

Consider the following excerpt from his most famous speech, delivered on June 5, 1944, to the troops on the eve of the invasion of Europe—D-Day. Notice the directness of the language, the emotional pull for his audience, the sentence patterns, the simplicity of the sentences and word choices.

> Men, this stuff that some sources sling around about America wanting out of this war, not wanting to fight, is a crock of bulls—t. Americans love to fight, traditionally. All real Americans love the sting and clash of battle. You are here today for three reasons. First, because you are here to defend your homes and your loved ones.
>
> Second, you're here for your own self-respect, because you would not want to be anywhere else. Third, you're here because you're real men and all real men like to fight. When you, here, every one of you, were kids, you all admired the champion marble player, the fastest runner, the toughest boxer, the big league ball players, and the All-American football players. Americans love a winner. Americans will not tolerate a loser. Americans despise cowards. Americans play to win all of the time. I wouldn't give a hoot in hell for a man who lost and laughed. That's why Americans have never lost nor will ever lose a war; for the very idea of losing is hateful to an American.

You are not all going to die. Only two percent of you right here today would die in a major battle. Death must not be feared. Death, in time, comes to all men. Yes, every man is scared in his battle. If he says he's not, he's a liar. Some men are cowards but they fight the same as the brave men, or they get the hell slammed out of them watching men fight who are just as scared as they are. The real hero is the man who fights even though he's scared. . . .

All through your Army careers, you men have b—ched about what you call "chicken sh—drilling." That, like everything else in this Army, has a definite purpose. That purpose is alertness. Alertness must be bred into every soldier. . . . There are four hundred neatly marked graves somewhere in Sicily all because one man went to sleep on the job.

In short, he knew his audience. He knew the emotional strings he had to pull to get them psyched to go into battle. Although I'm definitely not sanctioning his "eloquent profanity" as he referred to it, he did understand adapting his message to the audience and purpose.

Some people primarily take in information visually. Others pay attention to what they hear and rarely notice what they see. Still others learn and draw conclusions kinesthetically—primarily through what they experience through their own senses.

As individuals, people also vary along the continuum between the two extremes of directness—either very direct, bordering on blunt, or indirect, expecting others to read their minds. Their words will fall somewhere between a hint and a hammer.

In addition to individual styles, consider cultural

uniqueness. In high-context cultures the message comes not only from the words, but the context of the words: Who said it? When? How? In response to what? With what body language? What was not said? In other words, meanings are often implied and understood from many things other than mere words.

If unaware of such differences, you could insult people in high-context cultures by dressing too informally during an important sales presentation or management briefing or slouching in your posture. On the other hand, you can and should indicate status simply by greeting and introducing colleagues.

Edward Hall, a specialist in this area, ranks high-context cultures in this order: Japanese (highest), Chinese, Arabic, Greek, Spanish, Italian, English, French. In low-context cultures, the words themselves convey the primary message; the context carries less weight. Hall identifies the American, Scandinavian, German, and Swiss-German (lowest) among the low-context cultures.

Ignoring context can be a big mistake—in any culture. My first business trip to Malaysia almost turned into a disaster from the moment I stepped out of the airport. Because all the logistics of the trip had been handled through a third party, I wasn't sure exactly who would be meeting me upon arrival at the small private airport on the outskirts of the city—the client executive himself, a lower-ranking assistant, or a car service. A casually dressed man of middle age greeted me on arrival, having no difficulty at all recognizing me, the only blonde on the plane or in the airport at the time. We tried to make conversation, but his English was very limited, and I had learned only a few words of Malay. He held the door open to the backseat of his car, so I slid inside—as did my husband, who was traveling with me.

The man climbed into the front seat and drove us to the hotel in almost total silence—except to tell us what time he would be picking us up for dinner. At dinner, when he alone was our host, we realized that he must be the client, not a driver. Still, we wondered why he had been talkative (although not completely understandable in his broken English) inside the airport and had grown suddenly quiet during our ride to the hotel.

It took about three days for him to "warm up" to us. When I questioned the third-party sponsor about the icy reception, here's what he told us: "He thought you were showing him disrespect. He opened the back door of his car for you to ride there because women here always ride in the backseat. He intended for your husband to ride in the front seat with him. When your husband slid into the backseat with you, he felt insulted—that you were treating him like a driver."

The context determined the message. That was many years and miles of international travel ago. I've become a little wiser and much more sensitive in checking out such situations beforehand.

Although the American culture is considered a low-context culture, some people here still remain clueless about nonverbal messages that overshadow their words.

On consulting assignments, I've watched people walk into an executive boardroom to make a presentation, get an icy reception, and walk out with no idea of why the group did not sign off on their project. The reason may have been a cocky attitude conveyed through their posture, a laid-back attitude that showed in their lack of preparation, their disrespect shown through dress, or their irritation piqued in response to questions.

As an effective communicator, your challenge is to understand that context—and adapt your style to that of the other person to achieve your purpose. Otherwise, your conversation will prove to be as fruitless as trying to play a tennis tournament with someone who refuses even to return the ball.

Be Repetitious

Businesses run their ads for weeks, months, and sometimes years. Lawyers tell their story as they make opening remarks, as they question their own witnesses, again as they cross-examine the opposing witnesses, and as they summarize to the jury. Television sportscasters describe the play fans have just watched for themselves. Politicians insert the same talking points in stump speeches, debates, and campaign ads. Singers repeat the refrain after every verse.

Why? People hear what they expect to hear. They don't hear what they don't want to hear. To overcome that natural tendency to tune out, you'll need to repeat your message in multiple ways, at different times, using different methods to get your point across.

According to the latest research of what actually works to communicate a new strategy, for example, here's the drill:

► Provide regular updates on progress.
► Celebrate successes as they occur.

When someone says, "I don't get your point," adding detail doesn't necessarily do the trick. Consider the words, structure, context, focus, and frequency. If you get a blank stare, beware.

- ▶ Learn from failures along the way.
- ▶ Announce any changes as necessary.
- ▶ Discuss the new strategy in team meetings.
- ▶ Create a special newsletter to share success stories related to the strategy.
- ▶ Mention the topic at the start of every companywide meeting.

Repeat. Repeat. Repeat. Repetition drives retention.

CHAPTER 4

Is It Purposefully Unclear?

*You never really hear the truth from
your subordinates until after 10 in the
evening.*

—Jürgen Schrempp, former CEO
of DaimlerChrysler

I can't put off the decision any longer—I have to give the president an answer tomorrow about taking over the operations in Germany."

"Why would you turn it down? It'd be a great experience for your kids. Only two years there. Then you'd come back here and have any job you wanted for the next 20 years."

"It'd be great if it were just my wife and me. But I'd have to move our two youngest kids, my mother-in-law, and our granddaughter."

"The company wants you there, right? Did they give you a choice?"

"I think so—I mean, I *think* I have a choice. I guess that's what I'll try to determine in the meeting tomorrow with the president. He did *ask* me if I wanted the job."

"They don't *ask*. If you don't take this assignment, it'll be your last shot at the executive suite."

The manager with the pending meeting pondered his predicament: What had the president meant? Take it or leave it? Or, take it and love it?

The previous conversation on the mixed message unfolded between two managers in the front row of one of my seminars. We work, love, socialize, live in a climate where people don't say what they mean—even with the best of intentions.

If someone asks, "Hey, how do you like my new office?" you're not likely to say, "If I had to look at this color paint all day, it'd make me puke."

Families are no different. They often value polite conversation during a holiday weekend over direct discussion of serious issues. Some couples land in the divorce courts because neither can discuss straightforward feelings for fear of defensiveness from their spouse. The longing for harmony outweighs the importance of honesty.

> *To some extent, tact and evasion make civilization and camaraderie possible. But purposeful evasion as a rule, over time—where harmony is valued above honest communication—destroys trust, erodes morale, and lowers productivity.*

To some extent, tact and evasion make civilization and camaraderie possible. But purposeful evasion as a rule, over time—where harmony is valued above honest communication—destroys trust, erodes morale, and lowers productivity.

Six Communication Styles That Create a Climate of Either Paranoia or Productivity

Leaders typically fall into one of six patterns of communicating, and that pattern largely contributes to the communication climate of the whole team. Some styles are far more effective than others.

1. *Give and Let Live.* Leaders who use this style send out lots of information in all directions to everybody in the organization—regardless of whether it's tailored, relevant, or applicable to others' interests or needs. Their mindset: I've done my job in sending the information—let them figure out if they want to know what it all means.

2. *Sell and Compel.* Leaders who use this approach identify a few key themes, sell their point of view, and compel others to see the wisdom of their strategies and buy in to their goals.

3. *Align and Redefine.* These leaders listen for misunderstandings, continue to correct those who get "out of line," and redefine their goals. They rally the troops and ask them to "align" around those few core issues.

4. *Reply and Deny.* For the most part, these leaders play hide and seek and are seldom seen by rank-and-file employees and customers. They listen to the grapevine for questions, concerns, or complaints and then reply and either confirm or deny rumors.

5. *Control and Scold.* Leaders who use this approach withhold information in an attempt to control what happens. They scold employees, suppliers, and strategic partners, causing them to behave like dysfunctional family members. People pout, become jealous, backstab, become territorial, lie, tattle, play favorites, argue, withdraw, and generally work against each other.

6. *Share and Compare.* Leaders with this mindset communicate information and their conclusions drawn

about that information: their vision, goals, strategies, and initiatives. They ask for and listen to input from others before setting all decisions, policies, and plans in stone. Then they keep their ears to the ground for necessary course corrections as new information, better ideas, and varied viewpoints surface. They make as much effort to hear as to be heard, and they encourage other people to talk to each other about best practices.

> *Take a culture that values harmony above all else, . . . stir in an ineffective communication style of leaders, . . . and you have a recipe for dysfunction, desperation, and duplicity.*

Any one of the first five styles limits a leader's effectiveness and people's productivity. Take a culture that values harmony above all else, . . . stir in an ineffective communication style of leaders, . . . and you have a recipe for dysfunction, desperation, and duplicity.

Identify Mumbo-Jumbo Conversations in a Face-Saving Fiasco

Emotionally Immature, Defensive Employees

Delayed on a recent trip and sitting in an airline club for a few hours, I overheard this conversation between three thirty-something travelers. Amy, Jeanne, and Bill all arrived at the club together, piled their luggage in the chairs across from me, and began to unpack their laptops.

Bill offers to go out to buy hamburgers for all three. While he's gone, Amy and Jeanne discuss a customer presentation they've evidently just delivered in Chicago. Amy says to Jeanne, "I hate it when he critiques my presentations. He does that all the time. My slides. The structure. I don't think he's all that good himself. I thought I did fine today."

"Yeah, you did great," Jeanne responds.

Amy leaves to go get a cup of coffee and find a place to charge her cell phone.

Bill returns with the hamburgers and joins Jeanne. They unwrap their burgers and start eating. Bill gets interrupted immediately by a cell phone call. When he finishes the conversation, Jeanne asks, "Was that about the job? Have you decided who's going to get the promotion?"

"Yeah. Steve. I'm going to announce it on Monday. He did a fabulous job today in the meeting. We're sure to win that contract."

"Amy doesn't like it when you critique her on her presentations," Jeanne says. "She's intimidated."

"That's too bad. She could be so much better—if she got some help with those skills."

Jeanne nodded agreement and their conversation moved on to other topics before Amy rejoined them.

Two things struck me about that snippet of overheard conversation. (1) Jeanne told Amy what she wanted to hear—"You did great." (2) Amy had likely missed a promotion because she routinely rejected feedback from her boss.

But emotional maturity and openness to direct communication without defensiveness know no age boundaries. The following is an example of two senior vice presidents who stand in stark contrast in their ability to solicit and accept feedback.

I'd been working with a marketing group on a global conference they planned to host for their clients. After we selected the theme, shaped the message, and structured the various concurrent sessions, I began to coach some of the speakers.

After the first few coaching sessions, the director of the marketing team approached me and said, "Actually, after seeing the results with these guys, we think you need to work with the two executive vice presidents who'll deliver the kick-off and closing keynotes for the conference. Neither is exactly spectacular on his feet. If they can devote the time while you're here this week, would you be willing to stay an extra day and work with them?" I agreed.

The first VP—on vacation for the week—offered to come in for a day specifically to be coached. The second VP—on the seventh floor all week—agreed to come down for 10 minutes.

Feedback feels uncomfortable to many people. As long as face-saving remains the goal and culture, people will face a dilemma: Shall we be silent and save the relationship? Or communicate honestly and solve the problem?

Most of us like people who come right out and say what they think— unless they disagree with us.

—GRIT MAGAZINE

Underperformers

Allowing underperformers to remain on the payroll is a form of dishonesty that harms the entire organization. Continuing to pat them on the back and grant them raises does not square with their own reality. They know their work does not meet standards and does not match what their colleagues do. If you don't tell the truth about how they perform, how can they trust you to tell them the truth about other things?

Employees know which ones aren't pulling their own weight. When they're all treated the same and receive the same feedback despite the refrain "we reward people based on performance," they discount other promises as well. Trust dips even lower.

Great Performers Who Need to Grow and May Go

Some leaders fear complimenting their star performers. They figure if they tell these stars how well they're doing, they may develop their talents and move on.

What's worse? That they grow and leave—or become discouraged and leave? Without encouragement, the valued employees may feel that you don't care about them and leave to go where somebody cares more or will encourage them. Great performers need honest feedback as much as the underperformers.

Your Own Performance and Mistakes

A business development manager for a large oil company reported at the beginning of the year that he was about to close a large gas contract with a net profit of millions of dollars. When the deal started to fall apart, he couldn't bring himself to tell his colleagues that he had overstated the certainty of closing the contract. At the end of each quarter, he presented trumped-up, vague explanations about why the contract still remained unsigned—yet kept insisting that the deal would close "shortly." All budgets had been based on his projections. And when the deal did not happen, the loss of projected revenues created tidal waves throughout the entire organization.

When people have to admit their own mistakes, admissions often follow along these lines:

- ▶ "I was wrong, but so was everybody else."
- ▶ "What did you expect—under the circumstances?"
- ▶ "Well, I'm not at liberty to tell you all the behind-the-scenes things that happened, but we're fortunate things didn't turn out worse."

The message: Mumbo-jumbo meant to excuse the speaker's mistakes or failures. The attempt at face-saving rather than admission of error rarely works in the long run. Silent message: Self-protection at the expense of credibility for the long term.

Poor Performance of the Organization

Organizations report poor performance in lingo like this, excerpted from a recent press release: "Results were negatively impacted by reduced revenues and substantial costs incurred as a result of the wave of rumors and misleading press reports during the past quarter, as well as from uncertainties arising from our announced break-up plan, which distracted employees, customers, and vendors. . . ." Say what? Nice dodge. I dare you to find someone or a single thing to blame.

Other common explanations:

"... unexpected downturns in the market caused by several factors that gave rise to growing concern among our customers ..."

"... new competitors entering an already overcrowded and mature industry ..."

"... soaring labor costs and consumer unpredictability that have squelched profits ..."

"... growing unrest in global consumer markets causing pricing fluctuations and profit instability ..."

In short, the cause always seems to be external, vague, and, by any reasonable person's estimation, outside human control.

Unhappy Customers

Customers, too, find their way into these conspiratorial conversations. The conversation typically begins when a customer starts making demands outside the routine. The demands grow more and more bizarre until the entire organization becomes embroiled in the dishonest dialogue. "Sure, Mr. Customer, anything you want, Ms. Customer. We'll all walk on hot coals while balancing bowling balls on our noses, Ms. Customer. Of course that's not in the contract, but we'll be happy to add that on at no charge—we'll all just sell our firstborn to cover the cost."

The veterinarian owner of a local pet care clinic carried on such a conversation each time a particular customer, Mrs. Dimitri, came in with one of her cats. However, nothing the staff did pleased her.

On one particular day, Mrs. Dimitri called to make an appointment. When the receptionist mentioned her name, the staff conversation began again. What kind of scene would she create? Who would have not fed, shot, tagged, or brushed her pet the way she wanted—or would it be a new complaint this time? And who would have the "honor" of talking with her politely but dishonestly about it when she came in?

The office manager asked the doctor, "Can we fire this customer?" She replayed the conversations rumbling through the office, scene after scene of prior visits, until the vet okayed her plan. The office manager phoned Mrs. Dimitri and told her she'd be happy to have a copy of all her pets' records ready for her when she stopped by, but suggested she look for care at another clinic, "where they could offer the kind of pet care" she wanted.

"Absolutely not," Mrs. Dimitri insisted. "I love coming to your clinic—you provide excellent care."

From that day forward, she and the office manager began to have straightforward, honest dialogue when the customer discovered things weren't done as she expected them.

Decide to Be Direct Rather Than Play Dodge Ball

Difficult conversation stalls for many reasons: defensiveness, emotional immaturity, poor performance, fear of losing star performers, fear of admitting personal mistakes, disgruntled customers. Honest conversation leads to respect, accountability, change, and results.

Kind people sometimes confuse circuitous conversations with courtesy.

But direct language doesn't necessarily mean blunt, brash, or harsh. Clear can be courteous and respectful. Direct communication embraces rather than evades the truth, involves clear words, and focuses on the facts.

> *Kind people sometimes confuse circuitous conversations with courtesy.*

Eliminate Euphemisms
That Elude Meaning or Action

There is no wisdom like frankness.

—BENJAMIN DISRAELI

The absence of all the gory details makes everyday life civilized and bearable. Who wants to hear, "I need to go vomit up my breakfast" instead of the typical, "Would you excuse me, please, I'm not feeling well. I'll be back in a moment."

Who wants to hear, "A mugger ripped my cousin's guts out a few years ago and left him to bleed to death before anyone found him" rather than "My cousin was killed by a mugger a few years ago"?

Likewise, euphemisms have their place in social settings. "Our neighbors plan to downsize in the next few months" sounds more gracious than "Our neighbors are selling everything they can to raise cash and avoid bankruptcy." In a parent-teacher conference, the parents often hear, "Johnny is a natural leader" rather than "Johnny distracts the whole class with his antics."

But euphemisms complicate things at work: A manager says to her subordinate who continues to come to her with problems and for help with decisions rather than taking initiative on his own: "Jordan, I trust your judgment as a supervisor" when she means "Would you stop bothering me with such petty issues." Other examples may sound familiar:

- ▶ "His *vision* for this department is a little different." (Strange philosophy? Management style? Weird control policy?)

- "The *parameters* on that project might be expanding somewhat." (Headcount? Changing criteria? Adding objectives?)
- "We will consider *input from all sources* before we make final decisions." (What input? What sources?)
- "Several *contributing factors* may change the budget for next year." (Lawsuits? Competitors? Product defects?)
- "We'll base your bonuses on *enhancing the customer experience*." (Customer satisfaction scores? Faster checkout? More appealing décor? Cleaner environment when customers visit?)

Simply put yourself on the listening end of the project you're about to delegate: What comes to mind? If you draw a blank about your next action, not good. If you visualize a multiple-choice quiz and all answers seem either correct or incorrect, not good. The test item is flawed.

No matter the difficulty of your message, say it. If you want action, state it.

Explore the Facts, Not the Flaws

In a difficult conversation about someone's job performance, focus on facts, not character flaws.

Explore what has happened or is currently happening. Get the facts right. What should be happening? What's the standard or the goal? What action needs to be taken to bring about change? Who's going to take that action—you or the other person? No need to play psychiatrist or mind-reader, trying to decipher someone's intentions or analyze their childhood traumas. No need to discuss their eternal future—who will or won't live happily ever after.

Just tell it like it is about the current issue, happening, or habit—with respect and without malice—and ask for the specific change you need.

Purposefully unclear communication—with bad intentions or the best of intentions—can be devastating for both individuals and organizations. In such cultures, everyone gets along, goes along—and sinks together. Face-saving is rarely a good substitute for problem solving. Open communication and emotional maturity, rather than defensiveness, foster trust and excellence.

> *Face-saving is rarely a good substitute for problem solving.*

CHAPTER 5

Is It Consistent?

*Some people may doubt what you say,
but they will always believe what you
do.*

—Anonymous

Parents understand the dilemma that inconsistency presents to their children. Thus, the saying, "Do as I *say*—not as I *do*." Spouses who say "I love you" but fail to spend time with their mate end up in divorce court. Celebrities who say they appreciate their fans but never make themselves accessible to them eventually see their popularity wane.

Customers and employees experience the same disenchantment when they see inconsistencies in the workplace. As the old saying goes, you can't *not* communicate—by words, action, or silence. You communicate by

- ▶ the policies you enforce and the ones you ignore.
- ▶ the behavior you reward and the behavior you penalize.
- ▶ what you allow work time for and what you don't.
- ▶ where you spend your money and where you don't.

- ▶ where you spend your time and where you don't.
- ▶ the quality of the products and services you advertise and those you actually deliver.

As a leader, your challenge is to make sure everything synchs—what you say with what you do.

Understand Why People Leer at Their Leaders

During a time of falling stock prices, a large telecommunications company ran a full-page ad in the *Wall Street Journal* touting their customer support for their newest product. The headline on the ad emphasized how closely their software designers listened to what customers wanted.

A customer called the 800 number in the ad and got routed to nine different people and phone numbers through their automated system without ever talking to a live person. Finally, the voice mail of the ninth person referred the caller back to the original 800 number in the ad. A letter from the caller to the CEO suggested that inconsistency between their marketing hype and the day-to-day reality was the reason for the company's falling stock prices. That letter became an example in the organization's customer service training of "what *not* to do" in communicating to customers.

Individuals, too, have difficulty synching words and actions. For example,

- ▶ The manager who says he rewards people for outstanding performance—but then grants merit raises across the board at the same percentage
- ▶ The manager who says she values employee suggestions—but fails to respond to them

- The manager who espouses an open-door policy—but then beheads the bearer of bad news and terminates dissenters
- The manager who says empowerment is the key to staying close to the customer—but then requires five approval signatures for a $500 refund
- The executive who freezes raises because money is tight—but renovates the East Wing and adds an executive garage

Double-Check the Details

Last spring, we hired a 23-year-old college graduate with a 3.5 GPA as an administrative assistant. Molly (name changed to protect the naïve) impressed us during the interview process and insisted that she really wanted the job in her field of communication. Because business and technical writing is part of our course offerings to corporate clients, we pointed out to her that all our employees need to proofread everything carefully when communicating with clients because they notice errors and sometimes like to play "gotcha."

Molly proved to be a fast learner on all the software and procedures. Other than giving her a little help with punctuation, her supervisor considered Molly to be mastering the job quite well.

Imagine our surprise when Molly walked in on day nine and resigned: "I just don't think this job is a good fit. Commas, semicolons, spelling, typos. Those kinds of things just aren't all that important to me. They just don't matter."

If you sell shoes for a living, they probably don't. But if you're a knowledge worker, words are the commerce of ideas.

As coworkers alternately laughed and lamented Molly's comments and the wasted time in training her, I reflected on the bigger issue: the issue of attention to detail and commitment to accuracy in whatever work someone does.

Getting the right pills in the correct medicine bottle. Adding the passenger's name to the correct flight reservation. Adding the parenthesis in the software code. Putting the proper lug nut on the car wheel.

So that's what I asked about in the hair salon the following Saturday: Am I expecting too much for people to care about getting the job done right—that if we teach e-mail writing, our administrative assistant handling registrations should know where the comma or semicolon goes on the form?

The stylists on duty agreed and had their own story to tell. A new-hire there had been working six weeks; on average, she'd called in at least two days per week, saying she couldn't make it in on time to meet her appointments for one reason or another. The owner had had to cancel or shuffle all her clients to other stylists. Her tenure there was soon coming to an end for the same reasons—lack of commitment, inattention to detail.

My point is not punctuation, but attitude. Attention to detail reflects an attitude of quality, commitment, and consistency communicated to customers. When somebody says, "I'm not a detail person," I start to sweat.

You'll rarely hear this statement from chief executives. They're *always* "a detail person." The issue is *which* details merit their attention. They dive for details—the significant details—because they know details can sink or save an enterprise.

Attention to detail creates an overall message—one that's either consistent or not. And that message commu-

Attention to detail reflects an attitude of quality, commitment, and consistency communicated to customers. When somebody says, "I'm not a detail person," I start to sweat. You'll rarely hear this statement from chief executives. They're always "a detail person." The issue is which details merit their attention. They dive for details—the significant details—because they know details can sink or save an enterprise.

nicates volumes to others about the quality of work you expect from them.

Follow-Through—Do What You Promise

Carole took a six-month leave of absence from her financial services organization for medical reasons related to a stress disorder, and is now considering taking early retirement. Although she's a 25-year veteran and star performer, here's her story about the breakdown in communication with her boss:

The workload just kept getting heavier and heavier every week as they kept laying off people. They expected those of us who were left to keep picking up the slack. Several days of the week, I worked from home. And I logged onto the computer at 4:00 a.m. And there they'd be—hundreds and hundreds of e-mails. Every morning. Same thing. Hundreds more. Just waiting to be handled. And I'd work until 5 or 5:30 every night. Then go walk the dog and cook dinner. Then log back in about 7:30 and work until 10:00 and then log out and go to bed. Then log back in the next morning at 4:00 and do it all again. I'd tell my manager that we needed help in the department. There were only six of us left where we used to have 12. And my boss would say, "Yeah, yeah, well, just me know if you need any help with anything." Well, I *was* letting him know. He'd promise to get back to me with help. But he never did. I just couldn't take it anymore.

Carole's situation is not all that unusual. If we talked to the manager involved, he might tell us that his boss was saying to him when he asked for more headcount or larger budget, "Yeah, yeah, just let me know if you need help with anything."

The promises have to synch somewhere. If you say you'll send the report, send the report. If you say you'll call, call. If you say you'll arrange a meeting, arrange a meeting. If you say you'll add their name to the bidder list, add their name to the list. If you say you'll approve the funds, approve the funds.

Credible communicators follow through with what they promise—or stop promising.

Enforce the Rules You Write

You hear politicians say it frequently: We don't need more laws; we just need to enforce the laws we already have on the books.

The corporate version of that song? To be a credible communicator, apply the official policies you already have equitably across the board. If you say X is cause for dismissal and a favorite employee does X, you have to stand by your policy. If you say teams who achieve Z criteria deserve a bonus, and eight of ten teams meet the criteria, give the bonus.

Psychologists tell us that a good way to create confusion in children and destroy discipline is to apply rules inconsistently. For example, at 8 p.m. you tell the children it's time to go to bed but make no effort to get them there. At 8:15 they have made no move toward bed. You again insist that they begin picking up their toys and announce that they were supposed to be in bed at 8:00. At 8:30, you tell them you're "serious"—that it's past their bedtime. At 9:00, you finally turn off the TV and walk them to bed.

The next night, the same routine. And the next night. On the fourth night, at 8:00, you announce it's bedtime. They make no move toward bed. At 8:15, you go ballistic and spank them. Wrong move from night one. The children have been taught that the rules "on the books" are not to be taken seriously. Enforcement on day four "without warning" feels unfair.

Adults react the same way. Ever tried "staying up with traffic" on an interstate when the posted speed limit is 70 and everyone is driving 80? Have you ever had a patrol officer pull you over and give you a ticket, and you think, "Why me? Everybody else was going the same speed!"

No matter the players or the circumstances, inconsistency fosters resentment. Consistency in applying policies of any kind builds trust.

Reward What You Want

It worked for Pavlov. It works for parents. It works for the Pope. If people put forth the effort and get the results you want, reward them. Not every other time, not occasionally, but consistently. Sales managers know they can't keep a top sales team motivated if they keep tinkering with their compensation. Rewards count in most every area of life: Politics. Sports. Leisure. Entrepreneurial ventures. Religion.

Money is only one kind of reward. Other rewards include verbal pats on the back, leadership roles, increased responsibilities, reporting lines, recognition in front of customers and colleagues, satisfying work, visibility with important people, prestigious job titles, opportunities to work with and learn from more skilled people, opportunities to interact with more interesting people, travel, rest from travel, sabbaticals, training, or publication of ideas in white papers, articles, or books.

Let people know that they can count on you to notice—every time—and reward them consistently according to contributions that matter the most. Communicate appreciation and recognition by your rewards.

Live Your Lines

Embody your words. Demonstrate your values. High Point University (www.highpoint.edu), a small boutique college in High Point, North Carolina, with about 3,000 students, understands the concept well. In fact, University President Dr. Nido Qubein set about to completely revamp the image and physical landscape of the school by rewriting the mission statement of the university when he took the helm in January 2005. Their mission statement now reads, ". . . Every student receives an extraordinary education in a fun environment with caring people."

To live those lines, here's what he set about doing in the first 18 months there. First, he wants students and parents to feel welcome on campus. That welcome begins as soon as prospective students and their parents first visit the campus. The visiting student's name appears on the parking sign as he or she pulls into the campus parking garage: "Welcome, Susie Smith." Prospective student and parents get ushered to the president's office, where they meet Dr.

Qubein personally. And if he's away, they receive a DVD recording of his comments, apologizing for his being gone the day they visited.

On move-in day, rather than the typical dreary day that most college freshmen and parents experience in the summer heat, running up and down stairs with box-loads of snacks, sandals, and CDs, freshmen are greeted by upperclassmen who meet them at their cars to help them unload. They receive ice-cold bottled water and ice cream while they unpack. The president himself roams the campus shaking hands, meeting parents, and greeting wide-eyed students.

Safety surfaces as another concern on the minds of parents. Although crime is no more a concern in High Point than in any other small town its size, the school offers valet parking at the dorms after 9 p.m. as another way to communicate to parents that the school cares about the safety of its students and to eliminate that "eerie" feeling of walking across a dark parking lot alone at night.

Respect for the individual ranks high on the values list at High Point. Construction from all the renovation projects around the campus creates dust. So respect translates to a free car wash on Saturdays for the students.

Generosity places high on the values list as well. Kiosks serve free food—ice cream in hot weather, hot chocolate and soup in cold weather. Students learn generosity by seeing it modeled all around them.

Confidence, too, can be a boon to a student's career early on—both during academia and later. A bubble gum machine stands outside Dr. Qubein's office to encourage students to come by, pop in a coin, and have the courage to chat with the big cheese for a few moments about whatever's on their mind.

The total effect of Dr. Qubein's efforts to communicate

> *Model your words and values. Just as actors do, become the character that you play on the job. Better yet, make your role your autobiography.*

his values and "live his lines" at High Point speaks for itself. Donations at this private university during his first 18 months have been no less than an astounding $100 million—more money raised than in the previous 40 years. Freshmen enrollments have increased by 45 percent since he took over.

Model your words and values. Just as actors do, become the character that you play on the job. Better yet, make your role your autobiography.

Play to Stay

Socializing with the boss, colleagues, and customers sometimes presents an inconsistency. What someone sees on the job doesn't jive with what happens after 5. Consider these tips to make sure a couple hours on your social calendar at a trade show or holiday party don't crater a couple of decades of dedicated work:

▶ Make sure your humor is not hazardous to your health. You're judged not only for the stories you tell but also for those you think funny.

▶ Do not touch; do not pass go. Don't even think about it.

▶ Drink like your work depended on it—only moderately. Socializing with the boss or coworkers is no time to have one too many. Bury your troubles in the backyard if you must.

- Lead with your ears, not your mouth. Don't become a bore.

- Leave the gallbladder surgery and sales goals for another day. People want to know you have a life and can discuss topics other than business. But certainly they expect you to select topics appropriate for a business social setting.

- Make mama proud—mind your manners. They should be able to dress you up—and take you out.

In short, your life after hours should not shock those you lead 9 to 5. And even if coworkers prefer the party animal as project leader, that may not perpetuate the image you want to leave with your own boss or client. People want to know that your behavior off the job doesn't negate the values you communicate on the job.

As with overnight mail delivery, scheduled airplane departures, or your favorite restaurant meal—in every aspect of personal or corporate communication, consistency counts.

> *Most of us really want to be half-understood. Not to be understood at all is frustrating; to be wholly understood is humiliating.*
>
> —SYDNEY HARRIS

CHAPTER 6

Are You Credible?

*It's a shame when people can't
communicate. When they're managers
in your company, it's a catastrophe.*

—FORTUNE

It may be all about you. If people don't think you're personally credible, your message won't matter. And anybody who hides behind the computer all day and communicates primarily through e-mail or a Web site will be at a distinct disadvantage in building credibility.

Generally, five things either contribute or detract from people's inclination to believe you:

▶ *The Look*—your appearance and physical presence such as dress, grooming, body language
▶ *The Language*—the words you choose and how well you think on your feet to express yourself
▶ *The Likeability Factor*—your personality and the chemistry you create between yourself and others
▶ *Character*—your values and integrity
▶ *Competence*—your skill and track record of results

You can immediately see how electronic communication adds complexity to the equation:

▶ Anonymity of Web site postings, chat rooms, and e-mail puts character at question. Who's the real person posing behind the words?

▶ Chemistry is difficult to develop when you're "meeting" by video- or teleconferencing. Pity the poor person who's doing a job interview by videoconference. CEOs speaking by video to 60,000 employees face the same challenge.

▶ Body language and tone of voice are difficult to interpret in an e-mail.

▶ The polish that technology and media professionals require and contribute (makeup, scripts, teleprompters, coaches) often work against authenticity and informality that people really want to see.

Competence matters a great deal. People want to believe and follow a winner. When deciding to believe you, they consider carefully the old chorus, "If you're so smart, why ain't you rich?" We'll explore this concept further in Chapter 9. Character, too, plays a strong part in whether people tune in to what you say—in fact, it may be the deciding factor. Truth telling and consistency have their own chapters (Chapters 1 and 5).

Competence and character aside then, let's focus on the remaining three attributes of credibility: the look, the language, and the likeability factor.

The Look

Imagine yourself having run a couple of ads in Sunday's newspaper. One ad features a job opening for a chief financial officer. The second is a help-wanted ad for a janitor. When you arrive in your office on Monday morning, you see two people in the lobby, waiting for interviews. Do you draw some conclusions about which job each has come to discuss? Based on what?

Dress and Grooming—By Ice-T or Warren G.?

Lawyers tell their clients how to dress for a favorable jury verdict. Producers wouldn't think of shooting a movie scene if the wardrobe wasn't right. Consultants earn big bucks advising executives how to dress to win the confidence of Wall Street analysts and to woo investors.

Styles and suitability keep changing. If there's one fashion rule these days, it's this: "Anything goes." Ask around about the appropriate dress for a special event, and you'll likely hear someone say, "Don't worry about it—you'll see just about everything. Wear whatever you want."

Not only can that be a career-limiting move but that assumption as a long-term dress code can destroy credibility.

So how do you get it right? With the styles ranging from the likes of Ice-T or Britney Spears to the throwbacks of Warren G. Harding, what's a person to wear on occasions that matter most?

Three hints:

▶ Dress to feel confident, be comfortable, and cover yourself. And I'm not talking about wearing your pajamas or having your hair "natural" so that it falls in your face every time you move your head. But you don't want to be fidgeting with your clothes or hair when your mind should be on your message.

▶ Remove barriers between you and the audience. Don't show up at a beach resort retreat in a three-piece suit when everyone else is wearing shorts. Neither should you sport business casual when your client's culture considers anything less than a suit disrespectful or arrogant.

▶ Look successful at what you do. Dress in the best quality you can afford.

Body by Fisher

Plastic, whether Fisher-Price, Mattel, Hasbro, or Has Been, is out. Poise and presence instill confidence in your words. Make your body language relaxed, not rigid. Your posture, movement, gestures, and mannerisms should command attention when you speak but convey the message that you're approachable.

The larger the room or the audience, the bigger the gesture or the movement should be to underscore your message and connect with your audience. In general, gesture from the shoulder to have greater impact—up, out, big, away from the trunk of your body.

Your eyes convey the strongest message. Picture the closing two minutes of the presidential debates. The candidates look straight into the camera as it zooms in for a close-up. Just as actors, singers, and journalists before them, they are told to "make love to the camera." How well they do it can determine the presidential election.

The Language

Your language reflects your credibility in several ways:

▶ Word choice (formal, informal, inflammatory, precise, clear, specific, vague, general, profanity or the lack thereof, word fillers, proper grammar, jargon)

- Sentence structure (simple or convoluted)
- The ability to express ideas concisely and clearly both off-the-cuff and with forethought
- The ability to respond to challenging questions with poise, tact, and authority

For example, in a recent court proceeding, a lawyer continued to refer to automatic time and date stamps on database records of e-mail and phone calls as "memorializing" activities. Those who routinely use customer relationship management (CRM) systems as part of their standard office software understand that such database packages create time and date stamps automatically. The lawyer's word choice of *memorializing* conveyed his lack of understanding about how such software works.

That the CEO chooses to call someone's trip to the Middle East a "boondoggle" or an "investigative trip" provides clues about her stance on political donations the organization plans to make. In an assembly in which an employee asks a straightforward question, "Do you think employees should get paid for unused sick days?" you hear either a clear answer or a ramble that leaves you confused. When asked a hostile question, a manager responds either in like manner or with grace, charm, and even wit that leaves the other person wishing he'd never even brought up the issue.

Language showcases or cracks your case for credibility.

Decide: McDonald's or the Ritz Carlton?

Both venues have a place in our lifestyles. You dress in jeans and a sweater to have hamburgers at McDonald's. And you put on your best duds to entertain clients or celebrate anniversaries at the Ritz Carlton. You know what to wear and how to act at both places. The question is, where do you catch people being more "themselves"?

Stories like this circulate in chitchat and e-mails between coworkers:

- ▶ "John and I were just standing at the back of the auditorium, and the CEO walks up and is just standing around with us, shooting the bull—eating chili, talking about the ballgame. . . ."
- ▶ "I've met him—he's just a regular guy."
- ▶ "I got to talk to her once. We rode to the airport together. Her limo driver was picking her up, and I was just standing there with luggage, waiting for the shuttle. It was raining. And she said, 'Are you going to the airport?' and I said, 'Yes' and she said, 'Jump in.' She just asked me all about what we did in my department and how I like working there."
- ▶ "Just as I was leaving his office after the big presentation was over, something came up about the military. And I asked about his son. And we started talking about how proud he was of his service. We just really hit it off after that. Everything changed from that point on."

In our culture, informality is a big deal for many people. That's why radio and TV talk shows rank so well. People want to talk to celebrities "off camera," behind the scenes, presumably without their talking points, so we hear them respond spontaneously. Likewise, network news anchors are now hired as much for their ability to chitchat informally with each other, guests, and callers between the planned segments of the program as they are for their journalistic skills.

Informality is a big deal to many people because it feels warm, fuzzy, and believable.

Turn Off the Hard Sell

Movie stars bombard us with how many dollars their latest movie brought in at the box office. Brokers brag about how many billions of dollars in assets they manage. Management consultants tell us how many organizations they've pulled from the brink of bankruptcy.

Politicians can't take a question on a natural catastrophe anymore without using the occasion to push their agenda for the Middle East. When talking to Wall Street analysts, CEOs sound as though they're running for the Oval Office. Financial advisors explain estate planning as though they're auditioning for a slot as a talk show host.

People don't talk anymore; they "influence." Listeners grow so weary of it that they tune out the hard sell noise. Granted, the numbers count. Moviegoers, investors, and clients want to see the track record of whoever is talking to them—credibility hinges on competence as well.

But there's an off and on switch. People tune out when the switch locks into the "on" position 24/7. When it seems as though the whole world is trying to impress us, it's refreshing to interact with someone who's just trying to talk to us.

Be Authentic—with Praise, Questions, Greetings

Not all questions are meant to solicit answers. Often, they're meant to embarrass—and typically that's apparent to all in hearing range. The person with the red face and a weak answer, however, is not the only one left with a dent in his or her credibility.

Greetings and introductions, too, can appear to those watching from the sidelines like a photo op for the class yearbook. "Carlos, I'm familiar with you through your publications and have always admired your work from afar." "Nancy, it's wonderful to meet you. You've been a tremendous role model for all of us in the organization." "Tom, we're deeply honored to be with you tonight on this auspicious occasion to pay tribute to a man so richly deserving of this honor—a man who needs no introduction."

If these words start to roll off your tongue, stop them. Rephrase with a fresh thought that expresses authentic feelings.

Ensure Confidentiality

"Loose lips sink ships" appeared on World War II posters, signs, and barracks walls as a continual reminder to all that information falling into the wrong hands could have devastating effects. Idle comments can be almost as serious for civilians as soldiers.

As a leader in the course of assigning projects, you learn things about people, personalities, pet peeves, and priorities. Being "in the know" can tempt some to "let it go" to prove their powerful position. But people must feel safe sharing confidentialities with you. For the person concerned, one lapse can be the leak that drains credibility from everything you say in the future.

Leaders don't sink ships. They "batten down the hatches" and keep their mouths shut.

The Likeability Factor

To be heard, you have to make people like you. You need to create chemistry—with your staff as a manager, with your team as a project leader, with your boss, with your customer, with your strategic partners. People believe people they like. That's not a news bulletin.

Just as many roads lead to success in the workplace, many different personalities attract followers. But the following traits seem universally to attract people and open their minds and hearts.

Show Your Humanity—Be Vulnerable

In speaker training 101, people learn to tell failure stories before success stories. Generally, audiences have more in common with those who struggle than with those who succeed in life.

If you worry about whether your teen will graduate from high school without getting involved with the wrong group, say so. If your father-in-law drove you nuts during the holiday weekend, it's okay to mention to your colleagues on Monday morning that you might not have been the storybook spouse.

If you lose a customer, regret it rather than excuse it.

If you miss a deadline, repair the damage and catch up.

If you miss a payment, make it, with interest.

If you make a mistake, own up to it and correct it.

If you misjudge someone, apologize and make amends.

People respond to humans much more favorably than to machines. When you communicate with colleagues, never fear to let them see your humanity.

Be Courteous—Remember to Kick the Copier

Day in and day out, it's the small things that kill our spirit: The sales rep who empties his cold coffee and leaves the splatters all over the sink. The manager who uses the last drop of lotion and doesn't refill the container. The analyst who walks away from the printer, leaving the red light flashing "paper jam." The boss who walks into the reserved conference room in the middle of a meeting and bumps everybody out for an "urgent" strategic planning meeting. The person who cuts in line at the cafeteria cash register. The guy who answers his cell phone and tries to carry on a conversation out loud in the middle of a meeting.

Even the smallest courtesies kindle a fire that ignites chemistry and builds kinship. The courtesy of saying "hello" when you come into the office after being away. The courtesy of letting people know when you're going to be away for an extended period. The courtesy of honoring policies about reserving rooms, spaces, and equipment for activities. The courtesy of a simple "please," "thank you," and "you're welcome" for small favors.

Share a Sense of Humor

No matter whether people agree or disagree with George W. Bush's political positions, they typically admire his self-deprecating humor. At one of the Washington correspondents' dinners, that ability to poke fun at himself seemed to be the primary thing the media responded to favorably.

Bush said at the lectern, "I always enjoy these events. But why couldn't I have dinner with the 36 percent of the people who like me?"

At one such event, Bush even brought along his "double," comedian Steve Bridges, to make fun of his frequent mispronunciations. The double modeled for him one of his most difficult words to pronounce correctly: "Nu—cle—ar proliferation . . . nu—cle—ar proliferation. Nu—cle—ar proliferation." Then Bush tried it, "Nu—cle—ar pro-boblieration." The crowd went wild.

Self-deprecating humor can open hearts and minds to make people receptive to ideas in ways words alone cannot.

Show Humility

Power can be seductive. Praise pushes people's buttons, elevating peer pressure to feel important. And just as suddenly as lightning strikes, an act of arrogance can destroy an otherwise credible communicator. Refusing to acknowledge people when they speak to you. Failure to respond to people's suggestions. Haughty body language. Time spent only with those of your "rank and ilk" at a social gathering. An amused smirk in response to an idea expressed in a meeting. An upward roll of the eyes meant to discredit someone's comment in the hallway. A talk jam-packed with jargon meant to confuse rather than clarify. Insistence that things must be said one way and one way only.

Credible communicators show humility in innumerable ways:

> *Power can be seductive. Praise pushes people's buttons, elevating peer pressure to feel important. And just as suddenly as lightning strikes, an act of arrogance can destroy an otherwise credible communicator.*

- They let others showcase by delivering key messages instead of always having to be "on stage" themselves.

- They let others feel important by interpreting, passing on, and applying their goals and initiatives.

- They get input from others—and consider that input worthy of a response. (They don't ask for input unless they plan to consider it.)

- They excite others by asking for their help, cooperation, and buy-in.

- They share the limelight by telling stories about star performers other than themselves.

- They share leadership roles by telling success stories of other leaders.

- They communicate awareness and appreciation of the efforts and results of other people.

Certainly, credibility involves a balancing act between establishing a noteworthy track record and blending into the furniture. People do want to know that you know what you're talking about. But arrogance antagonizes them. Expertise tinged with a touch of humility goes down far better.

Your look, language, and likeable personality will have a huge impact on whether people accept what you say. If your message isn't sinking in, . . . if you're not getting the action you want, . . . maybe you should take it, well, . . . personally.

CHAPTER 7

Are You Concerned and Connected?

It is better to speak from a full heart and an empty head than from a full head and an empty heart.

—DUBLIN OPINION

After Hurricane Katrina, the worst natural disaster in the history of the United States, hit Louisiana, Marty Bahamonde, a FEMA employee on the ground in New Orleans, sent this desperate text message to Mike Brown, then head of FEMA:

Sir, I know that you know the situation is past critical. Here [are] some things you might not know.

Hotels are kicking people out, thousands gathering in the streets with no food or water. Hundreds still being rescued from homes.

The dying patients at the DMAT tent being medivac. Estimates are many will die within hours. Evacuation in process. Plans developing for dome evacuation but hotel situation adding to problem. We are out of food and running out of water at the dome, plans in works to address the critical need.

FEMA staff is OK and holding own. DMAT staff working in deplorable conditions. The sooner we can get the medical patients out, the sooner we can get them out.

Phone connectivity impossible.

More later.

Sent from my BlackBerry Wireless Handheld

Mike Brown's e-mailed response—his full response:

Thanks for the update. Anything specific I need to do or tweak?

Granted, we don't know of other e-mails previously sent. But what is certainly lacking in this response was concern—a response for which he was widely criticized.

Yet consider the irony of the following corporate clichés delivered to customers and employees every day:

- ▶ "Your call is important to us. Please hold for the next available representative. The wait from this point is approximately 30 minutes. Please do not hang up and redial. This will only delay your call."

- ▶ "Please sign in, update your insurance information, and be seated. Your name will be called when the doctor is ready to see you."

- ▶ "Please fill out the survey and provide us with your feedback. Someone will get back to you shortly."

- ▶ "Due to our current restructuring plans, it has become necessary to outplace 550 employees to right-size our organization. Those affected will be receiving an e-mail within the next 48 to 72 hours."

Although we have grown a little more accustomed to the sound of these comments, they don't exactly leave us feeling warm and fuzzy.

Connect with People as People

Leaders who show they care about people as individuals— not as employees, suppliers, or customers—make a connection. Those who don't not only fail to communicate but they also lose employees and customers over time.

A career officer tells of his decision to end his 10-year active duty army career and the rank of captain after a significant "mis-connection" with his career management officer (CMO). At his performance review, the captain discussed the options for his next career move with his CMO, who advised him to reenlist and laid out the steps for him to be promoted to major ahead of his contemporaries. The very next day following their discussion, the young officer, out of uniform, happened to pass his CMO walking across the parking lot. When the captain saluted and the older officer returned his salute and greeting, it was obvious he didn't even recognize the young officer—much less remember his name.

That was the moment that the younger officer made the decision to give up his 10-year career on active duty and join an organization where he could work for someone who valued his personal contribution.

How important is that personal connection for leaders? That captain signed on as a reservist for the next 20 years and made the rank of colonel, but he never forgot the lesson in leadership: connecting with soldiers as people, whether on the battlefield or in a parking lot.

It was that same communication principle that caused him to promise his old army buddy, John Cole, that he'd stop in to say hello to his daughter while touring her college campus, High Point University, 20-something years later.

And it was that same communication principle that spurred Dr. Nido Qubein, president of High Point University, where Hillary Cole attended, to arrange the meeting.

Why would Dr. Qubein go to the trouble? Eighteen months into his tenure there—with a $100 million fundraising effort just completed and renovations under way in every direction—why would he take the time to ensure that a 22-year-old former student-turned-employee have a chat with her father's old army buddy?

Connection is Dr. Qubein's natural communication style as a leader as well.

Here's how Hillary and her dad first connected with Dr. Qubein in John Cole's own words:

> After Dr. Qubein took over as president in Hillary's junior year, I quickly noticed a marked change. The buildings, the atmosphere, the campus—it all took on a new life. Hillary sent me a copy of his video series. And I began to listen to him on the way to and from High Point to pick her up. So the next time I was on campus, I saw him out walking, recognized him from his photos, and decided to introduce myself. I said, "Hi, I'm John Cole. I'm known by many titles, but *here* I'm just Hillary's dad."
>
> Dr. Qubein smiled, shook my hand, and said, "And around here *I'm* just known as the president of *Hillary's school*."

Dr. Qubein made a connection with a father's pride rather than focus on his own accomplishments.

Dr. Qubein also connects with students, staff, and faculty. Students receive a "Care Package" of goodies and snacks during exam week, accompanied by a letter that begins, "I hated exams, too, when I was in school ..." to let them know he understands their stress. He sends cards to staff and faculty on their birthday—again, to communicate that he values them as individuals.

Any student on campus can e-mail him with a concern and he responds personally. Recently, a student e-mailed to say her dorm room wasn't cleaned the day before. He had a box of chocolates sent to her room and e-mailed her an apology: "I'm sorry—we let you down. Please forgive us."

And that's why enrollment has taken a quantum leap at High Point University since Dr. Qubein took over the leadership role and why there's an excitement among the staff and faculty there.

Three leaders in their respective fields: The captain-turned-colonel. John Cole. Dr. Nido Qubein. Each has learned the secret of connecting as a habitual communication style.

Specifically, connecting with coworkers, customers, and staff might be as simple as remembering people's names, sharing airtime, letting them see your foibles, or just letting them know something of your personal life—whether it's the pain of your bunions or the pleasure of Uncle Mac's 100th birthday bash with all your family home for the weekend. That's often why blogs become so popular—the authors share their personal life (that their spouse likes French cooking or their teen just had a scuba-diving scare) along with their political philosophies or business tips.

Even though the majority of medical malpractice lawsuits are found in favor of doctors, experts advise that a dose of good old-fashioned bedside manner—spending more time with patients, answering their questions, returning their calls—would reduce such lawsuits. In short, connecting with people as people rather than connecting only as clients or coworkers will save untold time, energy, stress, and money.

Engage—Don't Just Report the News

Early in my career, I wrote an inspirational book based heavily on interviews. Having finished the first draft, I sent a few chapters to my editor and asked for feedback.

"Too much like a newspaper article," she said. "Where's *your* voice? I don't want a news story on what *they* said. I want your perspective on what *you* heard."

Many managers make the same mistake—they just report the "news," what they hear from their own boss. A senior executive from a large manufacturing organization called recently to say that they were having difficulty with those on the assembly lines "buying into" management philosophies, policies, and practices—even those geared to the employees' own safety and those that put money in everybody's pockets.

Later as the executives in the meeting explained it: "When we pass on news, information, or a change, the leaders themselves don't 'own it.' They just report it. And the way they pass it on makes it clear to their people that either (1) they don't fully understand it or (2) they don't support it." As far as I could tell from the symptoms of the problems, it was a correct diagnosis. No engagement—with the news or with the executives' point of view on the issues and no concern with how their staff would cope with the change in policies or procedures.

Harvard Medical School runs a program in which students shadow patients with long-term illnesses in order to better identify with their future patients. Concern is not a communication style easily learned.

In fact, according to many public relations directors, one of their greatest challenges is getting CEOs to move beyond logical explanations and address the emotional concerns of people. Whether CEO or assistant to the secretary, there's tremendous power in the ability to engage with people in a negative situation—rather than just report changes or hear bad news.

I remember renting a car in Harrisburg, Pennsylvania, one particular trip. It was a cold, dreary night, with blizzardlike conditions. After trudging to my car and loading my luggage, I discovered the car wouldn't start. When I turned on the ignition and the dashboard lit up, the gas gauge showed half empty. Then as I tried to pull the seat forward, a broken lever, along with a big glob of grease, fell off into my hand.

Fuming, I got out of the car, dragged my two bags back through the blowing snow, into the terminal. In a huff, I walk up to the counter. The rep says, in the most troubled tone, "Oh, no, what happened?"

I tell him.

"That's terrible. I can't believe we put you through that. Here," he reaches under the counter and hands me a bottle of cleaner for my hand. "There's the restroom; this cleaner will take that grease off. I'll have your new car ready when you come out. That's just inexcusable."

I go to wash my hands and return.

He says, "I've paged the service department to bring another car around to the front of the terminal."

We wait. They don't answer the page.

He tries paging them again. "This is ridiculous. I'm not

going to make you stand here while the service people try to find somebody. I'm going to get you another car myself. I'll be right back."

By the time he drove my car up in front of the terminal to meet me, I was calm again. Why? He sounded as put out with the service people as I did. He was fully engaged with the situation.

On the other hand, there was my stay at a major hotel chain, which had staffed the front desk with a robot in human form. The front desk staff couldn't find a package that had been shipped overnight to me. The package had arrived because a recorded message on the phone in my room reported the fact that the front desk was holding the package for me.

But when I returned to the front desk for the second time to retrieve it, the agent there still couldn't find it. "What exactly do you want us to do to make it right?" the front desk agent chirped robotically.

I explained for the second time that I just wanted them to look until they found the package. I watched as she glanced under the counter for all of 15 seconds.

She repeated: "I'm sorry, but we can't locate the package. What would you like us to do to make it right?"

I repeated my wishes: "Please find the package—look in the back. In your Lost and Found area. Wherever. Just look until you find it."

"I told you that we looked and we can't find it," she chirped. "And what exactly do you want us to do to make it right?"

"I want you to find the package."

I wanted engagement with my predicament. An attitude of concern. Both the hotel and the rental car agency made mistakes. But they generated two very different reactions from me—the customer.

Whether talking to investors about falling stock prices, to employees about pending mergers and job losses, to a staff member about a skill deficiency, or to a coworker about illness, don't just report information or the news. Be emotionally present. Consider the impact of the message you're delivering.

Never underestimate the power of engagement.

Phrase—Don't Blurt—News in a Sensitive Situation

The anxious family huddled outside the hospital surgical ward, hoping for the doctor to dash by on his way back into surgery on the older woman about to have her second open-heart surgery in less than 10 hours. Her first surgery had ended at 3:00 in the afternoon. The doctor had assured the family that everything had gone well and that she was on the road to recovery. Her husband and children had stepped into the Intensive Care Unit to see her for a brief five minutes.

At the 6 p.m. visiting time, the doctor would not permit the family to see her because a few of the smaller veins were starting to bleed and the nurses would need to watch her closely. At 8 p.m., the doctor reported that the bleeding was under control, that the patient was again doing well, and that he was going home for the evening. He recommended that the family do the same.

Within an hour, the situation changed again dramatically. The patient was wheeled back into emergency surgery—this time, the doctor opened her heart for the second time to retie all the veins coming loose after the first surgery.

As the concerned family stood in the waiting room, the doctor came out of the second surgery after midnight to report that things had gone well the second time around.

The weary husband, who had been keeping a vigil at the hospital for almost 24 hours, asked the surgeon, "What happened that she had to go through the roller-coaster afternoon and this second surgery?"

The doctor blurted out, "I told both of you in my office two weeks ago that 3 percent of all patients have these kinds of bleeding problems after surgery. She just happened to be one of the 3 percent."

The doctor turned and walked on down the hall.

Executives, managers, supervisors, and service agents often blurt out similar facts in the face of raw feelings. And their words hit others with the same thud.

Listen Like You Care

Acknowledge that you hear what others communicate to you—both verbally and nonverbally. Rather than interrupting or telling your own story, communicate concern through your words and your body language—good eye contact, appropriate facial expression, focused posture.

Acknowledging what someone says to you:

► "I certainly understand where you're coming from on that issue."

► "That's a big step you're taking."

► "That's a risky move—you must have second thoughts at times."

► "You must have felt proud of that accomplishment."

Probing, clarifying, or confirming as if you care:

- ▶ "So tell me your next step."
- ▶ "When do you think that you'll . . . ?"
- ▶ "What do you think caused her to do that?"
- ▶ "Why do you think he set that policy?"
- ▶ "So you feel that you really made the best decision under the circumstances, right?"
- ▶ "So what would you like to see happen in the next few years?"
- ▶ "In what ways do you think a mentor would help prepare you for promotion?"
- ▶ "What kind of outcomes do you think would be in your best interest in a situation like that?"

The following are *not* empathic comments—no matter how many times you've heard them around the watercooler:

- ▶ "It could be worse."
- ▶ "Looks like you'll just have to tough it out."
- ▶ "You think you've got it bad—you should hear what we went through last year."
- ▶ "This may be a blessing in disguise."

Listening means focusing on the other person with sincere, not just polite, interest—not just waiting your turn to talk.

> *One of the best ways to persuade others is with your ears—by listening to them.*
>
> —DEAN RUSK

Interpret Reaction According to the Context

A friend of mine, Sue Hershkowitz-Coore, tells the story of being on an airplane, headed home after a long week of travel. It had been a long hard day with several mishaps one after the other, including almost missing her flight, one she'd had to risk life and limb to catch in order to get home in time to make her son's baseball game. Just as she'd breathlessly fastened her seat belt and the plane had taxied away from the gate, the pilot announced a two-hour delay in takeoff, making it impossible for her to arrive home in time to see her son's game. Simultaneously, the flight attendant stopped by to ask, "And will you be having the beef or chicken tonight?" Sue burst into tears.

As people react to what you write or say, consider the context. Do they fear a pending merger? Are they already experiencing massive upheaval because of a merger? Is their comment in the wake of a layoff? Is their workload mind-numbing at the moment? Are deadlines looming large? Are they dealing with a personal problem that's adding stress to their workload?

What's true of people's feelings, opinions, or judgments today may change next week or next month based on the context. You'll not want to make long-term decisions and responses based on a person's short-term reactions.

Act on What You Hear and Report on What You've Done

The CEO of a large independently owned office supply and furniture company discovered the best way to compete with the national retail chains was to offer exceptional service. The focus of that service is listening to the customer with concern and taking immediate action.

Although the company had an exceptionally high accuracy pull rate (97.9 percent) even in the early years, occasionally, they made a mistake and delivered a dozen black staplers when the customer wanted a dozen gray staplers. So their policy was to tell the customer to hold the wrong order until the next delivery, at which time they'd pick up the incorrect order and leave the correct item. They calculated that it actually cost more to pick up some wrong orders than the items were worth. So in cases where the customer decided they didn't want a replacement item, they told the customer just to toss the item if they couldn't use it.

But their customer satisfaction surveys indicated this was an inconvenience—small customers thought these items were "in the way" during the interim while waiting to place their next order. The company listened—and took action, even though it cost them money to pick up wrong orders. Because this information from the surveys was so valuable to their operations and relationships with customers, they've continued to repeat these surveys and to report back to clients all the suggestions gathered—along with the actions taken on each suggestion.

Unfortunately, not everyone understands this principle of listening—and taking action.

A divisional director at a large telecommunications company left his organization after a stellar 20-year career to go to work for one of the distributors of his employer. The reason in his own words: "They have no concern for their people. Their managers would say, 'My department is going down. I need headcount. We're sinking. Help.' And the boss would just give the party line—'Work harder, call me if you need anything.' But they never made any changes based on the feedback they got from the field, no matter what the changing conditions were. They were just

> *Words should be used as tools of communication and not as a substitute for action.*
>
> —Anonymous

so slow, bureaucratic, and unconcerned. People and departments went down before they got any action."

Consider this: In our society, inaction equates to guilt and can often lead to criminal liability. If you know of a crime and don't report it, you can be charged as an accomplice. If you're a corporate leader and permit sexual harassment, the law holds that you are condoning such behavior. If you're a leader of a political party serving in Congress or the White House and fail to bring appropriate action against a colleague for misconduct, people expect your resignation or will demand your impeachment.

No action implies consent. Message sent: We don't care.

Apologize: Do It Wrong and You'll Be Sorry

Why won't the latest celebrity flap go away? Situations calling for a public apology come and go about once a month. Some rock star, movie actor, athlete, or politician gets caught shoplifting, driving while drunk, doing drugs, having an affair, uttering prejudicial slurs over an open mic, or taking a bribe, and the public becomes outraged about the duplicity. The public persona and principles preached don't match the private behavior.

What further enrages us about such situations is that typically the celebrity involved first takes the stance: "It's none of your business." When that line doesn't work, he or she tries to make excuses, "I was drunk/stoned/conned/didn't know that blah, blah, blah . . ."—fill in the blanks. When those excuses don't calm the waters, they finally come out with a belated apology. Life goes back to normal. We once again buy their music, see their movies, go to their ball games, or elect them to office.

There's only one exception to this rule: If the celebrity tries to offer a pseudo-apology, one with no real admission of wrongdoing. (For familiar examples, see Fig. 7.1). When that's the case, the media and public chew on the story until the celebrity spits out an admission of guilt. Only then does life resume for the wronged and the harangued.

Ditto at the office. People have difficulty offering an outright apology—an expression of "I'm concerned because I made a mistake/I did something wrong." And they get the same kind of reaction as celebrities do to their pseudo-apologies.

What makes a good apology?

1. *Admission of error, guilt, or wrongdoing.* The person accepts responsibility for what was said or done and its inappropriateness, inaccuracy, weakness, hurtfulness, insensitivity, or whatever.
2. *Specificity.* Apologizing specifically sounds sincere. Global, blanket apologies convey lack of concern or understanding of the situation or damage caused.
3. *Amends.* Apologizing typically involves some attempt to make things right, some words or gesture of goodwill toward the offended person or group.

Children learn these steps before they learn to count. But medical schools and hospitals are increasingly adding "How to Apologize" to their curriculum for grown-ups to learn as ways to head off malpractice lawsuits. According to a story by *Associated Press*, the hospitals in the University of Michigan Health System have been encouraging doctors to apologize for mistakes. As a result, the system's

Figure 7.1

Pseudo-Apologies That Alienate

Apology, Plus Denial

"No, I didn't e-mail the meeting agenda to everyone ahead of time. I apologize—I didn't know I was supposed to do that."

Translation: I'm not in error here. Whoever was in charge of telling me to do that screwed up—not me.

Apology, Plus Good Intentions

"I've been putting out fires all morning ever since I came in at 6:30, but I won't bore you with the details. So I apologize that I didn't e-mail the meeting agenda to everyone ahead of time."

Translation: I had good intentions, so please give me some credit for those. Besides that, I'm busier than most of you.

Apology, Plus Excuse

"I apologize for not e-mailing the meeting agenda to everyone ahead of time. It's just been my experience that nobody ever looks at them ahead of time anyway."

Translation: There's no reason to apologize then.

Apology, Plus Personal Problems

"I apologize for not e-mailing the meeting agenda to everyone. I think I told several of you about how my weekends have been going, so I hope you understand."

Translation: Please cut me some slack. I have personal problems.

(continued)

Apology, Plus Attack

"Well, I apologize for not e-mailing the meeting agenda to everyone ahead of time. Bill, Jean—did you have something you were particularly interested in having on there? Was there something you're not prepared to discuss because you didn't see this ahead of time? If so, we can postpone the meeting and reconvene tomorrow when you're more prepared."

Translation: You people are making a big deal out of a very trivial issue undeserving of an apology. Why are you trying to embarrass me? I can make you feel very small for bringing this up.

annual attorney fees, malpractice lawsuits, and notices of intent to sue have fallen dramatically.

An admission of wrongdoing isn't always appropriate, of course. But you can express regret over a situation, results, or an outcome no matter who or what caused it.

Failure to admit mistakes leads to outrage. Failure to express concern leads to bitterness. Survivors, even dying victims, forgive mistakes; they don't forgive unconcern.

Failure to admit mistakes leads to outrage. Failure to express concern leads to bitterness. Survivors, even dying victims, forgive mistakes; they don't forgive unconcern.

Concern connects people. In whatever situation—from product recall to layoffs to employee illness to accident victims to stressed colleagues—there's tremendous power in communicating your concern. When logic causes a lapse in the relationship, emotion closes the gap.

CHAPTER 8

Is It Current?

Language is the machinery of the new age.
—Don Watson, author of *Death Sentences:*
How Clichés, Weasel Words and Management-
Speak Are Strangling Public Language

*I*nstantaneous sums up today's standard for quality communication. Anything less seems inefficient. With one-hour dry cleaning, . . . 30-minute pizza, . . . drive-through car washes, . . . two-minute Lasik surgery, . . . digital photos downloadable in seconds, . . . ATMs spitting out cash faster than you can spend it, . . . instant-text messaging in syllables because words take too long, . . . bloggers protesting air strikes before the planes return, . . . why wait until tomorrow to find out who the new boss will be?

Speed in accessing information even suggests status. Show me a junior high student without a cell phone, and I'll show you a social outcast. Teens understand that being "in the know" dictates their social standing. If Brandi and Brad break up at lunch, those who don't know about it by the end of the day aren't in their social circle and won't likely be at the same parties on the weekend. It's true. Ask any teen you know if I'm not giving you gospel here.

The same scene unfolds in the workplace. Aside from the expectations raised by our Internet culture, the speed of passing on information one to one—Jill to Jeremiah, manager to staff, Bob in Accounting to Akemi in Engineering—makes people feel like family. For further evidence, tune in to the most popular TV sitcoms and see how often the storyline centers around the characters' personal lives at work. Their work colleagues have become their extended family. That said, when employees hear company news from outsiders—the media, a supplier, another company—rather than "the family," they feel betrayed.

Can you imagine turning on the TV tonight and discovering that your brother has been arrested on drug charges? Nobody from the family has bothered to call and let you know. Or, how about reading the newspaper and seeing a notice in the Obituary section that your cousin has died and no one has told you? Would you be angry? Hurt? Incensed? At least inquisitive as to why someone failed to notify you?

Similar feelings run through the minds of employees, suppliers, and customers when they learn of company events from an outsider—the newspaper, TV, radio, a blog, the next-door neighbor, or the guy at the gym, rather than from their own organization or boss.

The meaning of "outsiders," of course, varies. Sometimes Francine's boss tells the news to her department, news that Francine shares with Frank over lunch—whose manager hasn't even thought about telling his own staff. Result: In Frank's mind, by all rights, he has been wronged. His department has been "left out" in getting the family news.

The issues of speed and timeliness have become even more complex as hierarchies disappear.

Temporary teams are becoming more and more the norm—groups of bright people joining temporarily to work in cyberspace toward one specific goal. They link. They communicate. They work. They accomplish. They disband. So the plan for getting information to them has to be efficient and quick; otherwise, they no longer exist. They've been left out of the loop altogether.

Delay is deadly.

Everyday Operations: The Need for Speed

A few months ago, an account manager in our own office reeled from the bluntness of an e-mail from a would-be client when our server went down for six hours. When service was restored, the account manager immediately checked his in-box and found an e-mail from a prospective enrollee in one of our public workshops. He sent her an e-mail, answered her question, and apologized for the 6-hour delay because of the computer glitch. She zapped back a to-the-point response: "Too late. I've already enrolled in your competitor's seminar—someone who pays attention to their e-mail!!!!"

Expectations from customers grow higher and higher every week. According to a survey by Hornstein Associates, only 42 percent of businesses respond to e-mails within 24 hours. The federal government gives itself two business days to acknowledge and respond to phone and e-mail inquiries and up to 20 days to respond fully to "complex" inquiries (according to the Consumer and Governmental Affairs Bureau Web site).

Yet surveys show that a whopping 88 percent of customers expect a response within 24 hours, and 13 percent expect a response in less than an hour. Customers don't fare much better by phone. According to a study by the Portland Research Group, the average consumer has to call a company 2.3 times before having his or her issue resolved.

But beyond the numbers and the irate customers, consider your own colleagues. Waiting is not a favorite pastime. Delayed information typically means decisions are placed on hold, because nobody knows for sure which projects are in "go" or "no-go" status. Productivity takes a nosedive.

Delay decays morale.

Crisis: Speed or Consequences

A private task force, Business for Diplomatic Action, commissioned a study in order for businesses to learn how to communicate better in a crisis. The study, conducted by Echo Research in six global markets, reported by Robert Holland and Katrina Gill, found that 84 percent of the articles running in the international press following Hurricane Katrina were negative toward the United States. (No surprise, considering the tone of the articles here in the United States as well.) Seeing what happened with no plans, or at least minimal back-up plans for communication in a crisis, companies took note. The survey found that 69 percent of the companies that had a crisis communication plan used it during 2005 in response to some crisis.

In short, if you have a plan, you use it. If you don't, you suffer.

Specifically, getting information out fast helps you take care of people's immediate needs, address the rumors and concerns, and maintain morale.

According to the research done in the aftermaths of Hurricanes Katrina and Rita, FedEx serves as a model in crisis communication. They brought together a team of managers from several departments to coordinate both internal and external messages during the storms. They used e-mail, an internal satellite TV network, press releases to the public, Web posts, and telephone hotlines to update employees and customers alike and to keep operations running.

They also set up another stream of communication to take care of their affected staff in the area: what benefits they could access, how to get their paychecks cashed, how to access relief funds collected. Executives visited the areas to have face-to-face time with employees.

Contrast these efforts and those of other organizations that value speed in communicating with employees and customers . . . with the blame-game that went on for months and months among different governmental agencies about communication that *didn't* happen.

Terrorism. Need I say more about the need for speed—in gathering, coordinating, accessing, intercepting, and interpreting information, and then deciding and acting on that information?

When the government learns there's an attack planned involving the plane you plan to board,

When the government learns there's an attack planned involving the plane you plan to board, the building where you work, or the conference you're attending, how long do you want the powers-that-be to hold the information before releasing it to you? Although not always life-and-death situations, coworkers and customers have a similar angst about product or service defects.

the building where you work, or the conference you're attending, how long do you want the powers-that-be to hold the information before releasing it to you? Although not always life-and-death situations, coworkers and customers have a similar angst about product or service defects.

Delay can turn crises into disasters. And if the delay doesn't kill, maim, or destroy, at the very least, it infuriates people.

Nanoseconds or Nada

Start by having a crisis plan and let everyone know what it is. Then for the everyday communication, keep the following principles in mind.

Reduce the Volume

If the neighbors next door are always yelling, you won't pay much attention to a tirade at 2:00 in the afternoon. But if you never hear from them and then all of a sudden a blood-curdling scream wakes you at midnight, you're probably going to call 911.

The same holds true for your e-mail. The more people hear from you, the less they notice. If people typically read your information only "the morning after"—the morning *after* they were supposed to have attended a meeting, the week *after* they were supposed to have submitted a report, the day *after* they were supposed to have been on a teleconference—investigate why. Do people receive so much trivial, unnecessary, or related information from you that they ignore the vital?

If so, decrease the flow.

Prefer Substance over Shine in a Crunch

When faced with a time crunch, make it a habit to get the information out today in less-than-perfect form rather than wait until to-morrow for polished prose.

Do people receive so much trivial, unnecessary, or related information from you that they ignore the vital?

Wait too long to let people know what's going on behind the scenes and you set up the same disappointment that movie-goers experience when reviewers have already given away the ending.

And besides that, polishing the prose to perfection creates the perception that you're varnishing the truth.

Send Information at the Point of Relevance—or Not at All

I know, I know—this seems like an obvious point. But for some people, teams, and organizations, it must be harder than it looks. Otherwise, you and I wouldn't get:

▶ Customer satisfaction surveys so long after the service was performed that we don't even remember what the survey refers to

▶ Items so long after our request that we toss them upon arrival because we can't remember why we wanted them

▶ Calls from people who e-mailed or wrote to say they'd be "following up" and we have no recall of ever having heard from them before

- "Official" documents and certificates months after the proper paperwork has been submitted—and long after the need for them has come and gone
- Brochures months after stopping by to request information at a trade show booth—and long after we've already made a decision and purchase elsewhere

You can blame occasional late deliveries on a glitch in the technology. But when the message is oral, whom do you blame?

Blog with the Best

Blogging has become the answer to speed for many organizations—for both employees and customers. Currently, more than 40,000 new blogs are created daily. By the time this book hits the shelves, that stat will be outdated. In fact, experts are already predicting that blogging as a phenomenon has already peaked as the popular way to speed information to your employees and customers.

Whether bosses as bloggers is more than a current trend, no one can argue that blogging is a speedy way to communicate. Bloggers may post entries daily or even several times a day. Their readers can subscribe to those "feeds" and have those downloads dumped into their e-mail boxes immediately. Some of the more well-known corporate bloggers include:

- Jonathan Swartz, CEO of Sun Microsystems (www. blogs.sun.com/jonathan)
- John Mackey, president of Whole Foods Market (www.wholefoodsmarket.com/blogs/jm/)

- ▶ Bob Lutz, vice chairman of General Motors (http://fastlane.gmblogs.com/)
- ▶ John Dragoon, chief marketing officer of Novell (http://www.novell.com/company/blogs/cmo/)
- ▶ Kate Purmal, CEO of U3 (http://katesblog.u3.com/)
- ▶ Justin Rattner, CTO of Intel (http://blogs.zdnet.com/OverTheHorizon)
- ▶ Eric Blot, CEO of Awak'iT (France) (http://ericblot.blogs.com/eric_blot_awakit/)
- ▶ Jacques Kemp, CEO of ING Asia/Pacific (http://mycupofcha.ingblogs.com)
- ▶ Manoj Ranaweera, CEO of ebdex Ltd. (UK) (http://www.manojranaweera.com/)
- ▶ Tom Berquiest, CFO of Ingres (http://blogs.ingres.com/tomberquist)
- ▶ Mark Cuban, owner of the Dallas Mavericks (http://www.BlogMaverick.com)
- ▶ IBM staffers lead more than 50 blogs that discuss IBM products and general technology issues (http://www-03.ibm.com/developerworks/blogs)

In fact, Robert Scoble, a prominent former Microsoft blogger known in the blogosphere as "the Scobleizer," has made such a name for himself among the independent software developers who have a love-hate relationship with Microsoft that his departure from Microsoft in June 2006 made *USA Today*.

If you plan to put your efforts into blogging to get the word out fast, keep these key principles in mind:

- ▶ Make it personal; express your voice; take a stand on the issues you raise.

- ▶ Target your audience. Know whom you want to reach with your information.
- ▶ Know your purpose and why a blog is the best way to communicate with that specific audience.
- ▶ Allow feedback on what you say—the good, the bad, the ugly.
- ▶ Refuse offers from higher-ups, legal people, or corporate PR to edit what you say. To do so destroys authenticity. (Granted, editing may save your job or your hide in a liability suit, but that's another matter altogether.)
- ▶ Link to other resources for more information on your subject.
- ▶ Know when to shut it down. Blogs are not forever. They're meant to serve a specific purpose—let's say a specific policy or cause that you feel passionate about. When the issue passes, the blog has no further purpose. Start a new one to serve a different audience or purpose.

Some insist that bloggers have had such an impact on getting information out to the right people quickly that this trend has sounded the death knell for corporate PR departments. I wouldn't count on it. Accuracy still matters. But should you marry the blogger's speed to the research and precision of corporate PR, you'd take home a communication Oscar.

We're a culture of dedicated workers. Our ski jackets, backpacks, exercise bikes, kitchens, and cars, with their compartments for our iPods, cell phones, PDAs, speakers, and controls, accommodate our commitment to be connected. Being current, however, *doesn't* mean continually connected.

Speed alone—speed with distortion, for example—won't cut it. But communicating at the speed of molasses doesn't even count. Speed of communication serves only as a qualifier to enter the race for today's top talent and best customers.

CHAPTER 9

Does Your Communication Make You Look Competent?

The constant use of long, involved words proves two things: (1) that you're learned, and (2) that you're ignorant of how best to communicate with people.

—WILL CONWAY

People can't always follow you around to watch you fire a rocket, manage a research team, handle stubborn suppliers, or correct product-design flaws. But they do hear what you *say* or see what you *write* about that work. And they often judge your competence by what you communicate about your job—not necessarily by what they see firsthand.

Excuse me for paraphrasing a cliché, but you

> *Excuse me for paraphrasing a cliché, but you are what you write and say.*

are what you write and say. Your reputation with customers or colleagues often rests on a single interaction. If you have somebody else answer your phone, respond to your e-mails, or write your reports, they're creating that impression for you.

Creating Your Message: So What's Your Point?

You do have one, right? And a purpose? In any communication—whether a speech, e-mail, report, meeting, cafeteria poster, or trade show hospitality suite—identify your purpose: to inform, persuade, inspire, coach, commend, warn, entertain, introduce, overcome objections, respond to concerns, or answer questions.

Once you've determined your real purpose, you can shape your one-sentence message as a road map.

Make Your Message Sticky

Malcolm Gladwell, in his bestseller *The Tipping Point*, refers to contagious messages—messages that "catch on" as they're passed through the population. They become memorable because of their simplicity. Consider some of the most memorable advertising campaigns and political slogans in recent history:

- ▶ "Where's the beef?"
- ▶ "It's the real thing."
- ▶ "We'll leave the light on for you."
- ▶ "Are we there yet?"
- ▶ "Just do it!"
- ▶ "Real men don't. . . ."
- ▶ "Show me the money!"

- ▶ "Smile. Be happy."
- ▶ "I love New York."
- ▶ "Don't mess with Texas."
- ▶ "What happens here—stays here."
- ▶ "Man Law."

How important is structure and word choice? What if we changed these slogans and ads slightly?

- ▶ "Where's the beef?" to "Where's the hamburger patty?"
- ▶ "It's the real thing!" to "It's the old product we love."
- ▶ "We'll leave the light on for you." to "Our hotels and hospitality make you feel as though you're at home."
- ▶ "Are we there yet?" to "I'm tired of traveling—have we arrived?"
- ▶ "Just do it!" to "Act now—stop delaying."
- ▶ "Real men don't. . . ." to "Prove you're a man by. . . ."
- ▶ "Show me the money!" to "I don't do anything until I get paid."
- ▶ "Smile. Be happy." to "Life is easy. Relax."
- ▶ "I love New York." to "New York is a great place to live."
- ▶ "Don't mess with Texas." to "Don't litter across Texas."
- ▶ "What happens here—stays here." to "You'll have a great time in Las Vegas."
- ▶ "Man Law." to "This is an axiom generally accepted by men in all situations."

So what's my point? Take the time to make your message memorable.

Translate Concepts Like "Vision," "Strategy," and "Initiatives" to Specifics

If you're writing or speaking to an audience larger than one and using these vague terms, people are going to have different tasks in mind for their next week's to-do list. Vision in Asian corporations often refers to plans to be executed 20 to 50 years into the future while vision in American companies may refer to next quarter.

It's not just the lower-ranking employees you address who'll want more specifics. Political candidates receive as much criticism for vagueness on implementing their campaign promises as they do for their positions on controversial issues. People demand the particulars.

Remember That Facts Aren't Reasons— Don't Just Show a Scoreboard

Have you ever researched a "fact" on the Internet and found contradictory data? For example:

What's the literacy rate in the United States? According to the United Nations Development Programme Report 2005, the U.S. literacy rate is 97 percent. The U.S. Department of Education says it's 90 percent. The latest National Adult Literacy Survey in the United States reports it is between 77 and 79 percent.

How about holiday spending? Family Life Communications research firm says that the average U.S. household spends $490 each year on Christmas gifts. The National Retail Federation reports that the average consumer spends $738 on holiday gifts. MOPS (Mothers of Preschoolers) says that the average household spends over $1,000 for gifts during the holidays.

The fact is that facts can be false, wrong, misleading, or

misinterpreted—purposefully or accidentally. According to Mark Twain writing in his autobiography, "There are three kinds of lies: lies, damned lies, and statistics."

Even if a fact happens to be correct, it doesn't always double as a reason. For example, a salesperson may tell me that I can buy a caseload of off-brand PDAs for a special price of $99 each to give to key clients as a gift at the end of the year to express appreciation for their business. The salesperson may interpret that fact as a reason to make the purchase: a low price, a nice gift for clients. I may interpret that same fact as a reason *not* to make the purchase. No matter the special price, giving an off-brand to key clients may not create a good impression and instead may make my company look cheap.

> *Statistics are like witnesses—they will testify for either side.*
>
> —ANONYMOUS

Facts are just facts, until you interpret them as reasons "for" or "against" something.

Make Your Facts Tell a Story

The only thing worse than filling up your speech, slides, e-mails, or reports with fact after fact after fact . . . is not shaping them to tell your story. What story do your facts tell? What trail do the facts leave?

Tell how your division exploded with the introduction of the new widget, and your headcount climbed from 3 to 68 engineers in the first two years you were in business. Then tell how you grew lax in your quality control. Tell about your reject rates. Show how the customer satisfaction numbers plummeted. Show how orders started dropping off as fast as they were logged onto the computer. Then circle back to the

> *Numbers are the language of business. Unfortunately, it is a boring language when spoken by most leaders.*
>
> —BOYD CLARKE AND
> RON CROSSLAND,
> THE LEADER'S VOICE

layoff of 58 engineers three years later. Then out of the ashes came . . . Well, you get the picture. . . . Drama. Dialogue. Climax. Denouement.

Set the scene at the trade show. How many competitors were there? How many attendees? Of those, how many did your booth attract? Why? What was the attraction—or nonattraction? What did the competitor do to drive you nuts? What kind of lead follow-up/closing ratio do you have to do after the trade show to make your competitors eat dust?

Music, lights, camera, action. Facts alone will never feed the mind—at least not for long.

Create Impact with Stories

Captain Charlie Plumb, a jet fighter pilot who was shot down, parachuted into enemy hands, and held as a prisoner of war for nearly six years during the Vietnam War, tells a fascinating story. Several years after he was released from the POW camp, Charlie accidentally ran into the man who had packed his parachute! His story makes the point that none of us ever knows the impact we are having on the lives of others. And the point is so powerful that audiences remember it for years—even recapping it to their friends on the Internet and calling him years later to tell their own tales.

Whatever your message, stories will make it stronger: courage, determination, commitment, persistence, customer service, vision, caution, change. Consider all the stories that have created the rich cultures and legendary CEOs. There's the story about the employee who made a costly mistake at IBM that cost the company $10,000 who walked into CEO Tom Watson's office to offer his resignation. Watson's famous line: "Why would I want your resignation? I just paid $10,000 for your education."

Then there's the Disney story of Walt himself walking through the theme park, picking up trash. There's the story of Sam Walton driving to work every day with his lunch in a brown bag. There's the story of the Marriott bell captain giving a hotel guest his own shoes to wear for an early morning job interview.

As a teenager in my first job at Six Flags over Texas theme parks, I heard stories about hosts and hostesses being sent home from work if they got a drip of chocolate ice cream on their white tennis shoes. You can be sure we didn't show up with dirty shoes and disheveled hair if we wanted to be issued a uniform for the day and keep a summer job.

Such culture-creating stories still surface during my consulting projects. Perry, a financial advisor and now regional manager of a large brokerage house, encourages his trainees to use more stories in their sales presentations with clients by telling his own story of an earlier lost account. He was competing with another brokerage house for the 401(k) funds at a large hospital system in the Northeast. The hospital invited him and a competitor in to make a presentation to the group of employees, after which the employees could choose where to invest their 401(k) funds.

Perry walked in with all the facts on his side—better yields, better customer service ratings, wider fund choices, more flexibility in the plans. His competitor walked in with a better presentation. She focused on a few stories of how her company got involved in the lives of their clients, helping them to achieve their personal goals, particularly in times of crisis.

She walked away with 92 percent of the employee accounts; Perry, 8 percent. He attributed the loss solely to his competitor's use of stories to make her points memorable.

Two years ago I heard Colin Powell address an audience in Chicago, where he captivated the crowd—not with platitudes, statistics, and studies about leadership—but with stories of leadership and what makes America great. He ended with a story about a Chicago restaurant owner and a group of foreign exchange students who couldn't pay their dinner bill for the evening. Powell's point was that the generosity of America would best be demonstrated to the world individual by individual rather than through acts of government.

> *Never use a $100 story in a three-minute time slot to make a nickel point.*

Drive your point home with a well-chosen story. On the other hand, never use a $100 story in a three-minute time slot to make a nickel point. Make sure the point deserves a story. Consider carefully as you develop your message. Is your goal that of retention and impact? If so, create, shape, and deliver accordingly.

Use Analogies and Metaphors to Drive Emotion and Deepen Understanding

Analogies lead to a conclusion based on a specific comparison. Jeff Bezos, founder and CEO of Amazon.com, used this analogy in a recent report to shareholders: "Long-term thinking is both a requirement and an outcome of true ownership. Owners are different from tenants. I know of a couple who rented out their house and the family who moved in nailed their Christmas tree to the hardwood floors instead of using a tree stand. Expedient, I suppose, and admittedly these were particularly bad tenants, but no owner would be so short-sighted. Similarly, many investors are effectively short-term tenants, turning their portfolios over so quickly they are really just renting the stocks that they temporarily 'own.' "

We talk about "prime real estate" in referring to the home page of a Web site or placement above the fold in a newspaper or product catalog. Many Human Resource managers talk about "cafeteria" benefits to their employees. With just one word, this analogy implies that employees have a "menu" of benefits to select from, that a "parent" has agreed to cover the "total" invoice up to a certain amount, that employees select according to "taste or preferences" from that menu.

Such comparisons as these don't exactly solicit an emotional response; they simply clarify a complex concept.

Metaphors, on the other hand, imply a comparison and typically evoke an emotion and a mindset. Both types of comparisons can be succinct, yet powerful ways to manage how people think about an idea or situation.

If you wanted to make the point that someone was not fully engaged with his or her colleagues in a mission, you might use a war metaphor: "John ducks into his cubicle as if it were a foxhole. He needs to stick his head out occasionally and help the rest of us fight the war. Otherwise, the parent company is going to take over the entire department."

If you wanted to talk about how indifference to quality customer service could destroy your business, you might put it in these terms: "Our poor customer service has become a *cancer* eating away at our business. I see customers walk in here and wait 10 minutes before being greeted. Then once we do help them locate what they need in the store, they have to wait again at the checkout. Then they wait again at the loading dock. The longer a customer stays in our store, it's like our cancer metastasizes rather than goes into remission."

If you were making a point to your colleagues about the importance of living a balanced life, you might use a sports metaphor. "Most of us would agree life has many dimensions or tracks, all important to our overall well-being: mental, physical, spiritual. But some of us are spending all our time on one track and ignoring the rest, thinking we're going to find satisfaction and fulfillment along the way. It's not going to happen. That's like entering a triathlon and practicing only the bicycling for the three months prior to the race."

Author Malcolm Gladwell uses the metaphor of "contagious disease" in his bestseller *The Tipping Point* to describe how ideas gradually "catch on" and spread in the general population.

Metaphors and analogies, by their very selection, create a powerful way of thinking about an issue and often evoke a strong accompanying emotion that makes ideas memorable.

Take a Point of View

Avoid hype as a form of persuasion. But remember that the absence of hype doesn't mean the absence of opinion. Hired to help an investment company develop and shape their message, I listened to four executive vice presidents as they presented their segments of the "official" company overview. The General Counsel presented his overview of real estate investing and new regulatory laws relating to such. When he finished, I asked him, "Do you think real estate is a good investment for high net-worth individuals today?"

"Absolutely," he said. "The best. For several reasons." And he listed them for me.

"Why didn't you include those reasons in your presentation?" I asked.

"I did."

"I missed them."

"Maybe they didn't come across as reasons. But the facts were there. The investor could have drawn that conclusion."

"But why would you leave it to the listener to draw that conclusion?"

"Well, I'm a lawyer. I didn't want to come across as a used car salesman."

For the next hour, we discussed the differences between hype and a persuasive presentation. After all, his organization spent several million dollars annually flying in estate planners, financial advisors, brokers, and potential clients to persuade them to invest in real estate. Why would he not want to lead them to a conclusion?

Be clear about your purpose. If you're asked just to dump information, do it. But more often than not, you're expected to take a point of view about the information you provide. That point of view involves the four S's of persuasion to make sure all your listeners arrive at the same destination: solid facts, sound logic, straightforward language, and strong structure.

> *The four S's of persuasion: solid facts, sound logic, straightforward language, and strong structure.*

Hammer Them with Humor

I'm not suggesting that you become a stand-up comic. Just don't take yourself too seriously. If a funny story makes your point, tell it. If a one-liner says it all, toss it out there. If Sunday's comics capture your message, use them. Humor grabs attention, keeps people tuned in, elevates the energy level, and rewards people for listening all the way to the end.

Beware the Backdrop

Anticipate reactions to your message before you deliver it. Will their concern be money? Loss of face? A short deadline? Shuffling of priorities? If so, do you need to reconsider your phrasing? Add details? Clarify other issues? Consider the physical and emotional surroundings—the metaphorical context and timing—and modify your message accordingly.

Delivering Your Message: Split Personalities

Have you ever felt like interrupting a presenter to ask, "Is that you? I don't recognize your voice." The strangest thing happens when some people stand up to present ideas and information before a group—particularly an executive group. They sound like someone else.

It's as if they have two voices or communication styles. They have a talking mode and a "delivery" mode—and can move back and forth between them on cue. In their talking mode, they sound like a person engaged in conversation: natural, believable, engaging, connected, clear, animated, passionate, interesting. In their "delivery" mode, they sound like a robot: unnatural, stiff, disengaged, disconnected, complex, modulated voice, low energy, dispassionate, uninteresting.

My first challenge in coaching executives on their presentation skills is to bring these split personalities together—to help them learn to be their "natural" rather than "unnatural" self when speaking to a group. Whether speaking to a group, writing an e-mail, or conversing in the hallway, competent communicators have mastered these three parts of clear delivery: simple words, short sentences, specific language.

Here's an e-mail someone sent me, explaining his job:

> It is my job to ensure proper process deployment activities take place to support process institutionalization and sustainment. Business process management is the core deliverable of my role, which requires that I identify process competency gaps and fill those gaps.

What does he do? Why put your listener or reader in the position of decoding? Say what you mean. Nobody has time for this kind of puzzle. Save it for lounging by the swimming pool.

Make Your Bottom Line Your Opening Line

If you're telling a joke, directing a screenplay, or writing a TV sitcom, your audience will give you a few minutes to interest them before they yawn and walk away or flip the channel. Business colleagues aren't always that patient.

Audiences for your e-mail, your briefing, or your proposal want your bottom line up front for several reasons:

- It's difficult to understand the details if you don't have a summary of the big-picture message first.

- Attention wanes quickly. You'll need to grab listeners fast before they exit, nod off, or text-message their dentist.

- People expect applicable messages. With more than 500 TV channels to select from, 1,800 newspapers, hundreds of headlines, and blogs popping online faster than popcorn, people want to make their choices quickly.

> *When a speaker won't boil it down, the audience must sweat it out.*
> —ANONYMOUS

Whether good news or bad, competent communicators understand the value of getting to the point.

The first words from the moon: "Tranquility Base here. The Eagle has landed."

The first words of Winston Churchill after the fall of France during World War II: "The news from France is very bad."

The first words from President Bush's address immediately after 9/11/2001: "This is a difficult moment for America. . . . Today we've had a national tragedy. Two airplanes have crashed into the World Trade Center in an apparent terrorist attack on our country."

> *Many people who have the gift of gab don't know how to wrap it up.*
> —LIONS MAGAZINE

Get their attention by summarizing your message succinctly. Then follow up with the details.

Be Passionate

Take your personality with you when you present your ideas to a group or enter the conference room for a meeting. Sometimes people insist that they're afraid to be "too" anything—"too over the top," "too strong," "too overstated," "too sold on the idea," "too much the cheerleader." So in their quest not to be "too" anything, they lag in the land of "not very"—"not very clear," "not very sold on," "not very eager," "not very aggressive," "not very enthusiastic," "not very convinced," "not very sure," "not very prepared."

If I looked at someone with a "not very" personality and was asked, "Would you buy an idea from this person?" I'd have to respond, "No." How about you?

How passionate would you want your lawyer to be if pleading the facts of your insurance case to the jury? How passionate would you want your congressional representative to be in arguing for funding on research for your medical condition? How passionate would you be in persuading investors to fund your new entrepreneurial venture? How passionate would you be about pleading with a kidnapper to release your child?

Our passion rises and falls based on what's at stake. Your audience understands that concept all too well. They take their cues from you. Your interest interests them. The difference between "not very" and "too" can mean the difference between the life or death of your ideas and proposals.

Write Your Way Out of the Garbage Bin

E-mail in-boxes have become the postal boxes of a decade ago. They contain circulars, coupons, invoices, and the occasional greeting card. If your e-mail to others doesn't command attention, it gets deleted or dragged into oblivion with a click.

In my company's latest survey of 658 respondents from 20 organizations, here's what we discovered: Ninety-three percent receive more than 10 e-mails daily. Twenty-five percent receive between 30 to 50 e-mails daily. Another 24 percent of us receive up to 200 e-mails a day that have to be "handled." Seventy-nine percent say this glut of e-mail costs them at least two hours a day. Forty-seven percent say they're spending up to three hours a day handling e-mail. And one-fifth (21 percent) report spending four or more hours per day on e-mail. (See Figure 9.1.)

To compound the problem of a crammed in-box, many, if not most, e-mails are poorly written—often requiring a second or third reading. The biggest complaint, voiced by 47 percent of the respondents, is that e-mails are disorganized, irrelevant, or contain incomplete information.

Clearly, your competency shows up in someone else's in-box. The ability to write well not only documents your accomplishments—it also reflects your ability to think clearly.

A side note: Those who write better also make more money. Several detailed studies have shown a clear correlation between literacy and income. Of the 1,000 largest employers in the United States, 96 percent say employees must have good communication skills to get

This report, by its very length, defends itself against the risk of being read.
—Winston Churchill (Remark at a Cabinet meeting)

Figure 9.1
Competent Communicators Must Write Their Way out of the Garbage Bin.

Booher Communication Survey on E-mail*

The Glut Hitting In-Boxes:

71% report writing between 10 to 50 e-mails daily

23% receive more than 50 e-mails daily

Time Involved to Respond:

79% say they spend 2 hours daily on e-mail

47% say they spend 3 hours daily on e-mail

21% say they spend 4 or more hours daily on e-mail

Biggest Complaints about E-mail Received/ Opportunities to Excel:

Disorganized, irrelevant, missing information	47%
Too many	20%
Too long	18%
Poor grammar (unclear)	10%
Too technical	3%
Discourteous, blunt tone	2%

* Number of organizations surveyed: 20; number of respondents: 658.

---

ahead. Stephen Reder, a linguist at Portland State University in Oregon, has worked with the U.S. Department of Education in measuring how American adults' verbal proficiency affects their economic success over a lifetime. The results: Those in the highest quintile in writing ability earn, on average, more than three times what those with the worst writing skills make.

Forget the "Once Upon a Time" Format

"Once upon a time" opens many classic bedtime stories, but marks an amateur business document. Your clients, boss, or colleagues aren't reading for pleasure, so don't keep them in suspense. Start with "they lived happily ever after" or "we need your help to live happily ever after" (the overview message and action) and then circle back and give readers any necessary background details to take expected action or make a decision.

Recommend Rather Than Report

Those in staff positions, particularly, argue, "But nobody asked me to make a recommendation; they just asked me to answer a question."

Think again. In most such cases, the reason someone has asked the question is that you're the expert—the go-to person with the appropriate expertise. They don't want "just the facts, thank you, ma'am." They want your expert opinion. In light of the context, their goal, the question they've asked, and the question they *should have* asked, what's your recommendation to accomplish the goal?

When you go to see a medical doctor, do you expect an opinion along with your lab reports and X-rays? When you go to see your CPA, do you expect only the numbers or an opinion about what's deductible and what's not? When you talk to your financial advisor, do you want only a report on the effective yields of your portfolio or would you like the firm's opinions about various investments options?

Don't bring a problem and dump it at another's door as if to say, "There! I've done *my* part!" If you're the person most familiar with a problem and have the most information available, offer something actionable to move others closer to a solution. If you're the one battling in the trenches, what's your suggestion to others who can help? Communicate the next action as clearly as the problem and you'll certainly be labeled a leader.

Whether you're walking into the boardroom or the client's office, be ready to state a viewpoint or offer a recommendation. Consider that a key value you can contribute.

Know When to Blink: Fade Away Favorably

The head honcho strolls in late to a meeting, keeping everyone waiting. Or, she has the last word before a dramatic exit, leaving everyone scurrying to carry out the last command. Have an argument at home, and the same dynamic happens. The husband grabs his coat and exits with a terse, "I'm going to Atlanta." Done. Gone. So there.

The same dynamic happens in e-mail conversations when one writer stops responding. The implication is rejection: Done. Gone. I've more important things to do than e-mail you about silly little matters like this. Why don't you get on with your life and leave me alone?

On the other hand, you can feel a little silly carrying on an e-mail conversation like this:

"Our proposal to Universal is due on Friday. Please let me know when you've submitted it."

"I sent it out last Tuesday."

"Good. I'm hoping they make a decision before I leave for vacation next week."

"Yes, me too."

"Please copy me on any further correspondence with their proposal team."

"Will do. Sure thing."

"Thank you."

"Welcome."

So, when do you blink? What's the fine line between an exchange like the one above (that seems to suggest that you have way too much time on your hands) and the situation of not responding, implying that you're bored and they are beyond your point of interest?

Three quick tips to handle such a dilemma: (1) If the message is positive, assume all is well. If the message context is negative, spend the extra few seconds to reply and spare an offense. (2) Reduce the length of your response. A single word or phrase response implies "So long, I'm signing off now." (3) Repeat the action—yours or theirs. You're implying that one or the other of you should "jump right on it" and have no further time to e-mail.

Know What Never to Put in an E-mail

Ask any 10 people if they know of someone who has been terminated or an organization that has been hauled into court over an e-mail, and at least one can cite person and case. The story usually has an unhappy ending. Here are the no-no's:

1. Negative comments about executive management (Even if "deleted," these e-mails can be retrieved. Often such remarks accidentally get passed on. After four replies on an ongoing saga, someone forgets your sarcastic line buried at the bottom and accidentally forwards the e-mail to another colleague to answer a different question.)

2. Criticism regarding peer or staff performance issues (Written comments cause employees to brood. They seem more official than spoken words.)

3. Bonuses or salary issues (If positive plans fail to materialize, the writing seems like "proof" that they are deserved.)

4. Racial or gender slurs (Surely not in this century.)

5. Product or service liabilities (Opponents can subpoena your e-mails as evidence that you were aware of problems and ignored warnings.)

6. Competitor untruths (See you in court.)

7. Gossip about colleagues (Even the most innocent "news" can strike people the wrong way. If they want it told, they'll tell it.)

8. Sloppy writing (Clear writing reflects clear thinking. The opposite is also true. Your image may depend on daily informal e-mail more than on formal documents.)

9. Humor—particularly sarcasm and tongue-in-cheek (What comes across well with proper inflection, a smile, and a slap on the back frequently falls flat on the screen.)

10. Anything about your personal life you'd be embarrassed to have printed on the front page of your newspaper (Your love life, your weekend adventures, your political views. Nada.)

Pay Attention to Punctuation and Grammar

Consider the sad fate of the toothless tiger who zaps an e-mail like the following into your in-box:

Its come to my attention that several employee's have been parking in the Visitor Parking Lot in spite of regulations that prohibit that. We have sufficient employee space acrossed the street and violations of parking policy will not be excused or excepted. We have made this policy clear in recent staff meetings we will have security officers ticket those who park illegally. thank you for your consideration.

Power, power, power, who's got the power? Certainly not this manager. The person who sends out such an error-filled document becomes a laughingstock rather than a leader.

Incorrect punctuation and poor grammar can take you to court, cost you untold dollars, and even change the meaning of your prose. For example, the use of *may* and *shall* became a topic of discussion during the U.S. 2000 presidential election. Was the word choice in the election laws of the State of Florida a matter of inconsistency and ungrammatical usage or a correct and purposeful choice of words to convey strictly different meanings? Both George W. Bush and Al Gore made use of the grammatical arguments in their legal briefs filed in court.

The ability to write clearly is no small matter. Similar grammar issues determine the outcome of legal cases involving millions of dollars every day in corporate America. And, unfortunately, grammar determines clarity, rework, and productivity—whether supplies show up in Pittsburgh or Peoria.

Those who write and speak competently get attention. They earn promotions and respect as leaders.

Why? Your writing and presentations reflect your thinking: How well you organize your ideas. If you can sort the significant from the trivial. How quickly you think on your feet. How clearly and concisely you explain things and respond to issues, concerns, or questions. Part of what you do on the job stays off others' radar screens. But every day the world judges your competence by what you say and write.

CHAPTER 10

Is It Circular?

The true spirit of conversation consists
in building on another's observation,
not overturning it.

—*The Nazarene Preacher*

K ids learn early to play parents against each other: "But, Mom, why can't I go to the party? Dad already said I could!" The same communication quandary that families experience creates havoc at work.

Our general manager needed to renew our ERISA bond for our company's 401(k) plan. So she called the brokerage house that set us up with the mutual fund company investing our 401(k) funds to find the name of the person handling our account. The brokerage house told her they no longer have anything to do with our account—that they only set it up. They suggested that she call the mutual fund directly. She called the mutual fund. The mutual fund company told her they only invest the money; they referred her to their 401(k) fund "administrator company." She then called the administrator company. The administrator company said they knew nothing about ERISA bonds—except that the law requires that we have one. They suggested that she call their parent company—the brokerage company (the people she first called). Back to square one.

Lack of cross-functional communication within organizations is eventually exposed to the outside world: to customers, to suppliers, and to strategic partners. And it drives them nuts—if not out of business. Companies also lose employees because people don't talk to each other. Period. It's that simple. And that complex.

So what's circular communication? Communication going in all directions. Up the chain. Down the chain. Across departmental lines. From the day shift to the night shift. Feedback from the boss to the staff and vice versa. Conversation with customers. Feedback from customers. Customers talking to other customers.

For the most part, such communication doesn't just happen. At least, not routinely.

I still remember this nightmare from 20 years ago. In fact, I was so perturbed I wrote an Op-Ed piece (excerpted portion below) published in the *Houston Chronicle* at the height of the oil crunch, rising inflation, and 18 percent mortgage rates. It served as my explanation about why organizations lose money and customers. It's as true today as it was two decades ago.

> . . . We buy the house of our dreams and pull out the home-furnishings catalogs. Custom window coverings arrive from Department Store X. The master bedroom woven-wood is two inches too short and two inches too narrow. Someone didn't measure or record the dimensions correctly. Excuse offered: "I guess they didn't communicate the fact that they should come to the bottom of the windowsill." We send them back to the factory and reorder.

Humming to myself while the installer hangs the second set of woven-woods, I dream of privacy in the bedroom. But the installer comes down the hall shaking his head. "You wanted a double-pull wood, Ma'am? I'm afraid the factory made another mistake. Or someone copied down your order wrong again. I'm going to have to send this back, too."

On the third delivery, I am afraid to look. "Ma'am," the installer said, "you're not going to believe this, but they made the same mistake. It's the same one we sent back to the factory."

We begin to wonder, have we been singled out for this persecution? The second week after our move when mail dwindles to "Dear Occupant" circulars, a trip to the old address produces approximately an eight-inch stack of first-class mail.

Yes, various clerks responded, the Post Office does still have the change-of-address notice on file. But frequently a sub is on the route and possibly nobody has told him to forward the mail. The supervisor promises to "take care of it personally." Four months and numerous phone calls later, my husband resorts to removing the mailbox from the pole to stop the mail from going to the old address.

Anticipating such "disruptions of service," we had planned early phone installation: one month before M-Day, we had called to have telephone service transferred.

Four weeks later and before we have actually moved into the new house, the installer phones me at the old house. He wants to know where I am. He is at the new residence to hook up the phone and the house is empty. I tell him about the reschedule due to Mortgage Company X's foul-up, giving him name, date, and hour of rescheduling. He'd never gotten the word, he insists. "Somebody" had fouled up and not sent him the "reschedule" notice. We reschedule phone installation for a week later.

I wait in the new, cold, empty house for the installer to arrive between 8 a.m. and 5 p.m. At 4:55, he shows up.

We have a working telephone! But when I try to dial the downtown library, I can't. They have installed a limited suburban line instead of the metro service I'd ordered. "Sorry," he apologizes, "someone must have made a mistake in taking down the order."

Two days later, the phone bill arrives for one month's service. Since the phone has been working for only 46 hours, I call to complain. "Not to worry," the assistant tells me. She will adjust the bill and send a corrected copy.

A disruption-of-service notice arrives. I phone to say that I have never received a corrected bill. "We'll make a note not to disconnect then," the representative promises, "so don't worry." I do.

Two days later, the phone isn't working again. Our line is crossed with another. After 77 days we have a working phone.

A week later Customer Relations calls to ask about "the manner in which my recent order had been handled." I tell her, giving the names and dates of each conversation, miscommunication, and resulting foul-up. "This is my job," she gushes, "to catch problems like this. I'm going to give this to my supervisor for his personal attention and he'll get back to you immediately."

And . . . no one ever called back from Customer Relations.

Virtually the same communication caper surfaced again when our community bank merged with a large national bank and began bombarding us with paperwork, new PINs, and passwords—but couldn't coordinate their efforts during the actual changeover of their systems. For months we received paperwork saying, "Here's your new . . . ," followed by a call or letter telling us to ignore what we'd just been told in the previous communication. The next week, a new wave of misguided, uncoordinated communication.

The colossal internal communication collapse created chaos for their customers, as well as employees, for almost a year.

It's all too familiar, isn't it? The frustration of getting poor service because department X doesn't talk to department Y, . . . of people who don't listen, . . . of people not following through on what they tell you, . . . of telling companies who don't care, . . . of visiting Web sites that promise but don't deliver.

Companies who plan to be around in the next few years have to stop communicating like this—or shall I say stop *not* communicating like this.

The Problem Is Not the Problem

In most cases, as with the move across town, the problem is not the problem. The problem is not the technology. The problem is the *communication* about the problem. The lack of communication—either wrong or mishandled communication—about the problem causes more problems than the problem itself.

In the moving fiasco, consider these specific, individual communication mishaps: The window-covering people who didn't communicate the correct item numbers and specs to the factory. The postal letter carrier and supervisor who didn't communicate to replacements on the route. The telephone people who didn't communicate and coordinate service installation and correct orders between departments. The Customer Relations department who didn't communicate about the promised follow-up.

> *Circular communication requires a plan, patience, and persistence. And when those are lacking, profits and people suffer.*

Lack of internal communication—all of it.

Circular communication requires a plan, patience, and persistence. And when those are lacking, profits and people suffer.

We Don't Know What We Don't Know

The CIA, the FBI, and the Oval Office have been the butt of plenty of jokes in recent years for their failure to share intelligence. Yet we may be a nation of hypocrites for such finger-pointing. "Working in silos" has become the colloquial term for either hoarding information, forced isolation, or a personal decision to remain disconnected.

Meaningful internal communication involves true information sharing, not logjams in e-mail boxes. Far too often, we're circulating the unnecessary and hoarding the important. Not everyone understands the difference between volume and significance.

And not everyone wants to hear bad news. In fact, a survey by Sirota Survey Intelligence suggests that one-third (35 percent) of employees believe that their own companies do not encourage reporting vital information up the chain—even if it's bad news. Consider the difference between Churchill's and Hitler's nose for news.

In l941, Winston Churchill set up the Central Statistical Office as part of the Cabinet Office, with the official purpose of collecting coherent statistical information regularly that could be reported and accepted for use without question in governmental discussions. According to those close to him, he feared that people around him would spin the facts and not give him the straight truth—including the bad news.

Hitler, on the other hand, was not as perceptive about human nature. He surrounded himself with generals whom he mistrusted and who mistrusted him. According to historian Stephen E. Ambrose, writing in *D-Day*, "the generals' mistrust of Hitler was worth a king's ransom to the Allies."

When the Allied forces landed on D-Day, Hitler's generals dared not wake him from sleep to get the appropriate orders to move. Field Marshall Rundstedt concluded that the airborne landings were on such a large scale that they could not be a mere deception maneuver (as some of his staff argued). He wanted armor on the coasts to meet the attack. Ambrose writes: "Rundstedt's reasoning was sound, his action decisive, his orders clear. But the panzer divisions were not under his command. They were in [Oberkommando der Wehrmacht] OKW reserve. To save precious time, Rundstedt had first ordered them to move out, then requested OKW approval. OKW did not approve. At 0730 Alfred Jodl [Chief of Operation Staff in OKW] informed Rundstedt that the two divisions could not be committed until Hitler gave the order, and Hitler was still sleeping. Rundstedt had to countermand the move-out order. Hitler slept until noon."

A few hours later after giving his approval—after the German troops had lost precious time—Hitler walked into a state reception for the new Hungarian prime minister and other guests from Bulgaria, Romania, and Hungary, asking them to do even more for the German war economy.

Then after the meeting, Hitler still could not bring himself to tell the bad news. He spread out a map of France and told Goering, the Nazi propaganda minister, "They are landing here—and here; just where we expected them!" Although the prime minister had learned of the Allied landings at 0400, he did not dare speak up to correct Hitler's outrageous, blatant lie.

So much for the old adage "what we don't know won't hurt us."

Newspapers carry stories weekly of executives leaving major corporations to join small start-ups where they can reshape the culture by communicating their own values and philosophies. Employees join new organizations for the same reason: an atmosphere that values an open exchange of ideas and the chance to offer input and be heard.

We don't know what we don't know. But real leaders want to have input in making the communication culture better. They want to start or join a conversation.

> *Far too often, we're circulating the unnecessary and hoarding the important. Not everyone understands the difference between volume and significance.*

Lead from the Front Lines, Not the Sidelines

Leading from the sidelines is telling people what to do and watching to see that they do it. Leading from the front lines means deciding together with those involved in the situation what needs to be done.

Leading from the sidelines is reacting to what people tell you has happened. Leading from the front lines means taking charge of the situation.

Leading from the sidelines is talking to people about what they did wrong after the fact. Leading from the front lines means communicating about how to get it right the first time.

As a practice, leading from the front lines means you must be present with your team "in the thick of things." Listening to what people are saying. Asking questions. Chitchatting daily. Finding out what's on their minds. Getting their "take" on the situation. Asking for their input as situations develop. Communicating pros and cons as you make decisions and implement plans along the way.

> *It's much easier to be critical than to be correct.*
> —BENJAMIN DISRAELI

While it may be possible to control a group's view from afar, it's far easier to influence their thinking as you walk shoulder to shoulder than to shout commands from the sidelines.

Let Leaders Leak with Your Blessing

Let other people—your staff, your administrative assistant, your team leaders—pass on information rather than always being the one in the spotlight making all the announcements, leading all the meetings, and breaking all the news yourself. Briefing others ahead of time and letting them pass on information makes them feel important and part of the process. They'll have to answer day-to-day questions anyway, so you might as well fold them into the thick of the information process rather than keep them on the sidelines.

Spin Ideas Up

Those on the front lines typically suffer from the who-am-I-to-tell-you syndrome. If it's a new moneymaking or money-saving idea, the mindset is, "If I thought of it, surely you've already thought of it too." The result: Nobody passes the idea upward.

If it's bad news, the mindset is, "Hide it and it will go away." The result: Nobody corrects the problem until either it's too late or until delay makes the problem much worse.

Say and do something positive that will help the situation; it doesn't take any brains to complain.

—ROBERT A. COOK

If it's dissatisfaction, the mindset is, "They surely must already know about it and just don't care." The result: People stay and create trouble, or they leave and create a hole.

By anybody's observation, great ideas rarely rise to the top on their own. Leaders put systems and people in an open culture that spins ideas to the surface. Managing upward means spinning new ideas up to your boss as part of the value you contribute.

Make Your Motto:
"Who Else Needs to Know?"

Clients cancel orders. Suppliers change delivery dates. Partners change their capabilities. Salespeople leave the company. Accounting miscalculates invoices. Products get damaged in shipment. Things happen. And when they do, those "things" typically affect somebody else's paperwork, due date, delivery time, schedule, costs, budget, priority, work assignment, or staffing.

Make it a motto to ask "Who else needs to know," and a practice to notify all appropriate people right away when changes occur.

Publicize Your Point: Blog, Blast, or Blab

If you have kids, you understand that saying things once doesn't always do the trick. Repeat, repeat, repeat. Capture your message in a memorable slogan so that people pass it on—as they do a favorite movie or book title.

Also, make the media work for you: videoconferencing, Webcasts, print media, press releases, intranet postings, Web sites, voice-mail blasts, blogs, banners in the cafeteria, closed-circuit TV in the lobby, signs in the parking lot. Just get the word out. Of course, with people talking, blogging, and blasting, you'll expect to hear both agreement and disagreement with what's going on inside your organization. That's good.

Regardless of disagreement, Microsoft insists that blogging is one of the best things they've ever done to get their message out. Lenn Pryor, Microsoft's former "director of platform evangelism" tells of his earlier irrational fear of flying. A United Airlines pilot told him to tune in to Channel 9 from his plane seat, where he could listen in to the pilots' communications. After hearing real people talk honestly and openly about the situation in the air, he lost his fear of flying. He decided that Microsoft needed its own Channel 9—straight talk. That's when he hired famed blogger Robert Scoble to talk honestly online about Microsoft's successes and failures for the whole world to read. And that blogging by Scoble and others, according to Pryor, moved public opinion of Microsoft from a net negative to a net positive.

The negatives of such uncontrolled blogging? Negative comments may get aired to customers. People sometimes butt heads about someone's foul-up. People get fired when they go to extremes. Competitors may hear secrets. Liability can become a legal issue.

But the positives of publicizing your point in all directions far outweigh such issues: People will build relationships informally in all directions. Productivity goes up. You'll get things done efficiently—sometimes outside the regular channels. Internal heroes in your company will earn a good reputation with your customers and win their trust for the long term. And most important, employees engage.

For all the gripes against the government, kudos are certainly in order for this policy, highlighted by David Freedman in his "What's Next" column in *Inc.* The Federal Aviation Administration (FAA) rewards pilots who quickly report their errors, agreeing to waive punitive action if they report their errors themselves. Most pilots carry a self-reporting form with them in their flight kit "just in case." (Pilots are allowed only one "pass" every five years; crimes and crashes are another issue altogether.)

Why the policy? The FAA wants pilots to learn from others' mistakes so they can keep accident rates low. Self-reports from air traffic controllers, mechanics, and flight attendants flood in at the rate of about 3,000 a month. These reports and "lessons learned," selectively published in a newsletter, are required reading for 150,000 pilots and other aviation workers each month.

Freedman has singled out a few organizations bold enough to use internal blogs and databases for such purposes. Mayo Clinic, for example, has medical residents log their mistakes or any other problems they see so the hospital can analyze the errors and find solutions. The U.S. Department of Energy is pushing its contractors to gather and share goof-ups, and "lessons learned" databases are accessible to employees and all other contractors.

Is self-reporting of mistakes standard practice in your organization? Probably not. But can you imagine the value of creating a safe place for employees to learn from each others' mistakes?

Publicize your positive messages, of course. But also motivate people to join any conversation that matters; this will eventually result in improvements.

Publicize your positive messages, of course. But also motivate people to join any conversation that matters; this will eventually result in improvements.

Make Feedback an Obsession

Look into your lover's eyes and whisper, "I love you" and what do you expect to hear in return? Silence? If it happens often, the relationship's in trouble. Yet every day that awkward silence can be "heard" when people say to a boss, "It's done" and hear . . . silence in response. In one survey of 1,727 respondents, only 47 percent of employees reported receiving feedback at least once a week.

Fully 81 percent of more than 1,400 leaders, managers, and executives participating in a study conducted by The Ken Blanchard Companies, a California-based consultancy, cited their failure to provide appropriate feedback, praise, or redirection as a personal shortcoming. Yet, 43 percent of these same leaders identified communication skills as the most critical skill they needed to succeed!

> *It's a toss-up as to which are finally the most exasperating—the dull people who never talk, or the bright people who never listen.*
>
> —SYDNEY HARRIS

What we expect and what we want—and what we get and what we give—seem to be very different things.

Why is that? Back to the lover analogy. As long as your lover leans close and whispers, "I love you," it's easy to respond with "I love you, too." But let the lover say, "You have bad breath," and the response he or she is likely to get will probably not be "I love you, too."

In his groundbreaking book *Working with Emotional Intelligence*, researcher Daniel Goleman reports that his surveys of American employers reveal that employers don't give feedback because people can't take criticism. They get defensive or hostile. They react to job feedback as though it were a personal attack. So leaders clam up and employees become no wiser about areas for growth.

And the higher you go in an organization, the more difficult it is to get honest feedback. Instead, you're surrounded by people who have everything to gain by commenting on your strengths, and who fear they have everything to lose with a negative comment.

The message here? If you're serious about getting feedback, you have to take matters in your own hands. If others give feedback hesitantly, make it more comfortable by asking key questions either periodically or after you complete key projects: "What ideas do you have for making this project even more successful next year?" "What would you change if you were handling this project next time?" "You're pretty good at synthesizing information—what is the consensus of opinion about how this project went?" "I'm always interested in self-improvement. What skills would you add to my 'needs improvement' list for the next 12 months?"

Organizations, too, have to assess where they stand internally and externally with customers. Interviews, surveys, focus groups, online audits, exit interviews—all paint the picture. The findings of the Sirota Survey Intelligence of 370,378 employees also showed that when people don't think employers treat them with respect they are more than three times as likely to leave their company within a two-year time frame. What do people consider as demonstrations of respect? Being recognized for accomplishments. Soliciting, listening to, and acting on their ideas and suggestions. Encouraging full expression of ideas without fear of negative consequences. Providing helpful feedback and coaching.

Without feedback in marriage, lovers drift toward divorce. Without feedback at work, employees drift toward the door.

Take the information you gather in such feedback sessions and develop your personal or corporate action plan. Without feedback in marriage, lovers drift toward divorce.

Without feedback at work, employees drift toward the door.

Cultivate Compelling Conversations

Think how often you replay conversations in your head—what you've said or plan to say to someone. Consider conversations a learning tool. They teach you both intellectual and emotional truth. That said, use them to create circular communication.

Bring people together. Be thought provoking. Start watercooler conversations to improve processes, save money, make money, discover new markets, or innovate. Find new places to talk to get the creative juices flowing.

Resolve conflict productively, but don't squelch it. Level the playing field to generate good debate and input, but keep the power balanced. These comments will come in handy: "Give these people a hand for opening the door on a new suggestion." "We'll need to thank Teri and Carlos for pointing out our blind spot on this issue—this could have cost us a lot of time down the road." Set the ground rules so that others learn how to respond constructively to diverse opinions, without interrupting, minimizing, and attacking.

Most important of all, don't let a quick wit turn into a sharp tongue that shuts down the whole conversation. Avoid being the resident gloom-and-doom critic or the Pollyanna who placates but fails to support the ongoing dialogue.

> *Don't let a quick wit turn into a sharp tongue that shuts down the whole conversation.*

Create value and recognize value in those who influence others to think.

Lead Work Sessions—Not Bull Sessions—
When You Meet

Humorist Robert Orben quips, "The two biggest problems in America today are making ends meet—and making meetings end." According to our Booher survey, 51 percent of the respondents attended on average more than four meetings per week. Of those meetings, one in five lasted longer than an hour.

And what's the payoff for that big investment of time? Not much. According to these respondents, 29 percent report that they accomplished the meeting goal less than half of the time.

So how can you turn bull sessions into productive meetings?

First, get the right people in the room. Make sure the people who have the key information get invited to the meeting. Otherwise, you have pooled ignorance. Who are the key influencers? Who can veto decisions made in the meeting? Who will likely oppose decisions and plans made in the meeting? Whose cooperation do you need to make sure all decisions are implemented? These are the people you need in your meeting.

Put together an appropriate agenda in the form of a focused question, not an issue. Far too many meetings have as their stated purpose things like "Philadelphia Trade Show." Does this mean you're going to discuss whether to attend? Determine the budget for the show? Identify ways to attract visitors to the booth? Decide whether to have a hospitality suite? Decide

> *To have an open mind doesn't mean you must always have an open mouth.*
>
> —ANONYMOUS

what product lines to show? Outline your marketing before the show?

You get the idea. Topics do not an agenda make. Topics simply tempt attendees to tiptoe through the issues lightly and leave with nothing decided. Instead, focus the topics into key questions that should be answered by the end of the discussion. As facilitator, close the meeting with assignments and follow-up action. Be known as the person who gets things done rather than the person who just *talks* about getting things done.

Meet, greet, lead, . . . discuss, decide, disband.

Know When to See the Whites of Their Eyes

As you encourage information exchange at all levels, you'll need to make a critical decision often. What's the best approach? E-mail? Phone? Or a face-to-face conversation? A formal letter or report? The method you choose can make a tremendous difference in results (Figure 10.1a).

After gathering input on these issues for years, I've compiled a chart of the consensus about which methods work best in which situations for what purposes (Figure 10.1b). Select at your peril. Above all, decide by design, not default. Don't make it a haphazard "Oh, by the way, while I've got you" happening in the hallway on Friday afternoon at 4:00.

Learn to Connect All Along the Food Chain

In a culture that encourages conversations at all levels, you may find yourself talking with everyone from the CEO to the chauffeur. Be ready to connect at *their* point of interest. When talking to people up and down the

Figure 10.1b

The method of communication sometimes determines the success of the message and the outcome of the situation. Decide by design, not default.

Email, Phone, or Talk Face to Face?

Reasons/Situations for Face-to-Face Conversations

▶ Immediate feedback or reaction (in body language/voice tone)

▶ Concern about the privacy of comments (can't be recorded/passed on)

▶ Expression of importance/extra time involved (an apology, bad news)

▶ Negotiate details on sensitive issues

▶ Persuade the disinterested/uninterested—to arouse interest

▶ Give mild reprimands

▶ Build a relationship (regain trust, create first impressions)

Reasons/Situations for Phone Conversations

▶ Listen and show that you've listened

▶ Need to hear someone's voice tone to "read between the lines"

▶ Negotiate details

▶ Persuade the disinterested

▶ Give mild reprimands

▶ Make sure "how you say it" is as precise as "what you say"

Reasons/Situations for E-mail

▶ Unavailable in "real time"
▶ Complex information that will warrant repeating or rereading
▶ Easier, faster distribution to many recipients
▶ Productive use of uninterrupted time
▶ Need a "paper trail"
▶ Less expensive than a phone call
▶ Faster than regular mail and "phone tag"
▶ More to-the-point messages than when pleasantries exchanged otherwise

Reasons/Situations for Formal Memos, Letters, or Reports

▶ Strong image with customer/partner
▶ Perceived as protocol in some situations (company introduction)
▶ More formal announcements (new product launches, price increases, reporting data)

food chain, you can build a bridge by asking, "What are some key projects on your radar screen this month?" "What kinds of things are giving you headaches this week?" "What are you most proud of this month?" "What's going well for you?" "How can I help you get things done here?" "How do you spend your time when you're not working?"

Their responses will lead to common interests, goals, concerns—or at least questions or issues you can ponder.

Time spent putting out communication wildfires takes time away from making a profit and accomplishing a mission. Do you have that time to spare? If not, circular communication may be your biggest untapped resource and greatest competitive advantage. Talk it up.

A Final Note

Communication makes the "top three" in many lists today. The most important ingredient in happy marriages. The most essential element in raising well-adjusted teens. The most vital skill in job-interviewing success. The greatest problem voiced by political parties in gaining support for their candidate. The most frequent complaint employees cite as their reason for leaving an organization. The most frequent reason top talent joins a new team. The biggest challenge leaders experience in times of change and upheaval. The most critical component of great customer service.

It's all about communication. And success in business is all about how well you communicate—to your coworkers and customers. So the next time you face a dilemma about what to say, when to say it, or how to say it, mull over these possible perceptions or realities and consider these strategies:

Perception or Reality	Strategy
Either you're not being completely forthright with them—or they think you're not. They don't trust you.	Tell the straight truth.
They're getting incomplete information.	Give complete information—all you know.
They don't understand what you mean. Your message is unclear.	Write and speak simply and clearly.
You're being purposefully evasive to save face—yours or theirs.	Be direct. Avoid double-speak—for whatever reason.
What you're saying seems inconsistent with what you're doing.	Make sure your actions, policies, and behavior match your words.
They don't consider you credible —either you don't look or talk the part or they don't like you.	Strive to be personally credible—in your appearance, in your language, and with a pleasant personality.
They think you don't care about Connect them personally. They don't feel a connection with you.	Communicate your concern. with people individually and as a group.
You're slow to communicate. They've heard important information from somebody else—and they feel wronged because you didn't tell them first.	Be responsive. Communicate important messages—even bad news —quickly.
They think you're incompetent in your job because of weak communication skills.	Write well. Speak well. Others will judge your competence in many areas by these most visible skills.
They're working in isolation, with no opportunity for input or feedback.	Encourage open discussion and feedback in all directions—up the chain, down the chain, across functional areas, and with customers.

As you put these strategies into practice, you'll hear "Why is there no communication around here?" less and less often. Instead of complaints, cover-ups, and blame, people will be buzzing with inspiration, ideas, and innovation.

Endnotes

Page 5, ... *than lip service to the idea* ... Thatcher, Mandy. "Challenging the Status Quo in Senior Leader Communication," *Strategic Communication Management,* October/November 2005, pp. 6, 9 (study by Melcrum on leadership communication).

Page 10, ... *companies with ineffective communication practices* ... Finney, John. "A World of Difference," *Communication World,* July–August, 2006, pp. 34–36. (Source: Watson Wyatt 2005–2006 Communication ROI Study, involving 335 participating companies in the United States and Canada)

Page 11, ... *dangerous corporate culture* ... Charan, Ram, and Jerry Useem. "Why Companies Fail," *Fortune,* May 27, 2002.

Page 19, ... *The International Association of Business Communicators* ... Anonymous. "Bad News Bearers," *T+D,* March 2006, p. 60.

Page 20, ... *second most often reported offense* ... Thibodeau, Jan. "Course and Discourse." *TD Journal,* August 2006, p. 13. (Study entitled: "The Business of Truth: A Guide to Ethical Communication")

Page 37, ... *according to the results of a study of 1,845 U.S. workers* ... Kornik, Joseph. *Training,* October 2006, p. 20.

Page 49, ... *effectively communicate their goals* ... Conway, Joe. "Senior Leaders Improve Their Communication with Employees, Towers Perrin Consortium Finds," TowersPerrin.com Press Release: Stamford, CT, September 7, 2005.

Page 75, . . . *here's the drill* . . . Speculand, Robin. "Getting Employees Behind Strategy," *Strategic Communication Management,* February/March 2006, Vol. 10, Issue 2, p. 5.

Page 121, . . . *identify with their future patients.* Thornburgh, Nathan. "Teaching Doctors to Care," *Time Canada,* 6/19/2006, Vol. 167, Issue 25, pp. 46–47.

Page 121, . . . *emotional concerns of people.* Martin, Dick. "Gilded and Gelded," *Harvard Business Review,* October 2003, Vol. 81, Issue 10, pp. 44–54.

Page 131, . . . *to sue have fallen dramatically.* Soll, Roger, MD. " 'Sorry' Seen as a Magic Word to Avoid Suits," *Associated Press,* November 15, 2004.

Page 135, . . . *to e-mails within 24 hours.* iMediaConnection.com by eMarketer, May 4, 2005.

Page 135, . . . *response in less than an hour* . . . Greenspan, Robyn. "Customer Service Lags, CRM Spending Expectations High," *E-Commerce Guide,* April 4, 2003.

Page 136, . . . *before having his or her issue resolved.* Jekl, Jason. "Putting Customer Back in Customer Service," Supplement to *KM World,* November/December 2005, p. 58.

Page 136, . . . *in response to some crisis.* Holland, Robert J., and Katrina Gill. "Ready for Disaster?" *Communication World,* March/April 2006, pp. 20–24.

Page 137, . . . *face-to-face time with employees.* Cagle, Jimmy. "Internal Communication during a Crisis Pays Dividends," *Communication World,* March/April 2006, pp. 22–23.

Page 141, . . . *made* USA Today. ——"Irreverent Blogger Leaving Microsoft." *USA Today,* June 12, 2006.

Page 153, . . . *that they temporarily 'own.' "* Bezos, Jeff. Letter to Shareholders, Amazon.com, 1998.

Page 161, . . . *with the worst writing skills make.* Fisher, Anne. "The High Cost of Living and Not Writing Well," *Fortune,* December 7, 1998.

Page 175, . . . *even if it's bad news.* ——"Bad News Gets Easier," *T+D,* November 2005, p. 16. (Staff written)

Page 180, . . . *a net negative to a net positive.* Scoble, Robert, and Shel Israel. *Naked Conversations,* Hoboken, New Jersey: Wiley, 2006, p. 18.

Page 181, . . . *at least once a week.* Laff, Michael, "Got Stress?" *T&D,* July 2006, pp. 28–36. (Survey: Joanne Sujansky, CEO, KEYGroup Consulting)

Page 182, . . . *skill they needed to succeed!* Weinstein, Margery. "When Leaders Go Wrong," *Training,* August 2006, p. 11.

Page 182, . . . *it were a personal attack.* Goleman, Daniel. *Working with Emotional Intelligence,* New York: Doubleday/Bantam, 1998, p. 12.

Page 183, . . . *within a two-year time frame.* Durett, Jacqueline. "R-E-S-P-E-C-T: Find Out What That Means to Employees," *Training,* June 2006, p. 12.

Bibliography

"Achieving Organizational Goals," *Healthcare Executive*, vol. 21.3, May/June 2006, p. 56.

Allen, Beverly, "A Culture of Communication," *Human Resources Professional*, vol. 21.1, Feb./Mar. 2004, p. 34.

Audhesh, Paswan K., "Perceived Managerial Sincerity, Feedback-Seeking Orientation and Motivation Among Front-Line Employees of a Service Organization," *Journal of Services Marketing*, vol. 19.1, 2005, pp. 3–12.

"Bad News Bearers," *T+D*, vol. 60.3, Mar. 2006, p. 17.

"Bad News Gets Easier," *T+D*, vol. 59.11, Nov. 2005, p. 16.

Baldoni, John, *Great Communication Secrets of Leaders*, McGraw-Hill, New York, 2003.

Banja, John D., "Empathy in the Physician's Pain Practice: Benefits, Barriers, and Recommendations," *Pain Medicine*, vol. 7.3, June 2006, pp. 265–275.

"The Best Methods of Internal Communications," *Business Communicator*, vol. 6.4, Sep. 2005, p. 2.

Bird, Shelley, "Counseling for Communication Leadership," *Communication World*, vol. 22.5, Sep./Oct. 2005, p. 31.

———, "Communicating Through Changes in Leadership at NCR," *Strategic Communication Management*, vol. 10.1, Dec. 2005/Jan. 2006, pp. 30–33.

Booher, Dianna, *Communicate with Confidence! How to Say It Right the First Time and Every Time*, McGraw-Hill, New York, 1994.

———, *E-Writing: 21st-Century Tools for Effective Communication*, Simon & Schuster, New York, 2001.

———, *From Contact to Contract*, Kaplan, New York, 2003.

———, *Speak with Confidence*, McGraw-Hill, New York, 2003.

Borrus, Amy, "The SEC: Cracking Down on Spin," *BusinessWeek*, issue 3952, Sept. 26, 2005.

Bossidy, Larry, and Ram Charan, *Execution: The Discipline of Getting Things Done*, Crown Business, New York, 2002.

Burton, S. Keith, "Without Trust, You Have Nobody: Effective Employee Communications for Today and Tomorrow," *Public Relations Strategist*, vol. 12.2, Spring 2006, pp. 32–36.

Cagle, Jimmy, "Internal Communication During a Crisis Pays Dividends," *Communication World*, vol. 23.2, Mar./Apr. 2006, pp. 22–23.

"Chief Humanising Officer," *Economist*, vol. 374.8413, Feb. 12, 2005, p. 64.

Clark, Boyde, and Ron Crossland, *The Leader's Voice: How Your Communication Can Inspire Action and Get Results!*, SelectBooks, New York, 2002.

"Communicating via Hidden Channels," *The Business Communicator, London*, vol. 6.8, Feb. 2006, p. 2.

Cory, Lloyd (Ed.). *Quotable Quotations*, Victor Books, Wheaton, Illinois, 1985.

Edwards, Catherine, "On Being Gregarious," *People Management*, vol. 12.8, Apr. 20, 2006, pp. 32–34.

Eigen, Lewis D., and Jonathan P. Siegel, (Eds.), *The Manager's Book of Quotations*, AMACOM, New York, 1989.

Ekroth, Loren, "The Future of Conversation," *Journal for Quality & Participation*, vol. 28.4, Winter 2005, pp. 18–20.

"E-mail Culture May Harm Business," *Engineering Management*, vol. 14.5, Oct./Nov. 2004, p. 4.

"Enabling collaboration at IBM," *Strategic Communication Management*, vol. 9.5, Aug./Sept. 2005, p. 4.

Field, Anne, "What You Say, What They Hear," *Harvard Management Communication Letter*, vol. 21.1, Winter 2005, pp. 3–5.

Field, Anne, "Are You Giving Your Top Performers a Reason to Stay?" *Harvard Management Communication Letter*, vol. 3.2, Spring 2006, pp. 3–5.

Finney, John, "A World of Difference," *Communication World*, vol. 23.4, Jul./Aug. 2006, pp. 34–37.

Fischhoff, Baruch, "Getting Straight Talk Right," *Harvard Business Review*, vol. 84.5, May 2006, pp. 24–28.

Freedman, David H., "What's Next: Mistakes Were Made," *Inc.* magazine, Oct. 2006, pp. 65–66.

Fugere, Brian, Chelsea Hardaway, and Jon Warshawsky, *Why Business People Speak Like Idiots*, Simon & Schuster, New York, 2005.

Gallagher, Rollin M., "Empathy: A Timeless Skill for the Pain Medicine Toolbox," *Pain Medicine*, vol. 7.3, June 2006, pp. 213–214.

Gingras, Marcel, "The Great Communication Challenge," *Canadian Manager*, vol. 30.4, Winter 2005, pp. 9–10.

Goodman, Ted (Ed.). *The Forbes Book of Business Quotations*, Black Dog & Leventhal Publishers, Inc., New York, 1997.

Gould, Victoria, "Making Communication Part of the Plan at Morgan Crucible," *Strategic Communication Management*, vol. 10.3, Apr./May 2006, pp. 18–21.

Grates, Gary F., "Supporting a Business Renaissance at General Motors," *Strategic Communication Management*, vol. 8.2, Feb./Mar. 2004, pp. 14–17.

Hansen, Fay, "Employees Doubt Credibility of Communications," *Compensation & Benefits Review*, vol. 36.3, May/June 2004, p. 24.

Hanson, Kim, "Should the Boss Be Blogging?" *Strategic Communication Management*, Vol. 10.2, pp. 6–7.

Hardage, Ginger, "Profile: Communicating the Southwest Way," *Strategic Communication Management, Chicago*, vol. 10.3, Apr./May 2006, p. 4.

Hetzel, Melissa, "Better Communication Can Prevent Lawsuits," *Cosmetic Surgery Times*, vol. 8.3, Apr. 2005.

Hillert Jr., Martin A., "You Should Be Committed," *Management Quarterly*, vol. 47.1, Mar. 2006, pp. 34–37.

Hobson, Neville, "Not-So-Small Talk," *Communication World*, vol. 23.3, May/June 2006, p. 16.

Hochhauser, Richard, "Communications Is Key to Happy Customers," *Industry Week*, vol. 254.13, Dec. 2005, pp. 30–31.

Hoogervorst, Jan, "Implicit Communication in Organizations: The impact of Culture, Structure and Management Practices on Employee Behaviour," *The Journal of Managerial Psychology*, vol. 19.3, 2004, pp. 288–311.

"How Can Communicators Help Build a Good Reputation?" *Business Communicator*, vol. 6.4, Sept. 2005, pp. 1–2.

"How to be Effective in the Five Major Areas of CEO Communication," *Business Communicator*, vol. 6.3, Jul./Aug. 2005, pp. 10–11.

Huber, Jurg, and Peter Boyle, "Roche's Holistic Approach to Leadership Communication," *Strategic Communication Management, Chicago*, vol. 9.6, Oct./Nov. 2005, pp. 18–21.

Johnson, Susan M., "Innovative Communication Program in the Spotlight," *Management Quarterly*, vol. 47.1, Mar. 2006, pp. 26–32.

Kornik, Joseph, *Training*, Oct. 2006, p. 20.

Laurence, Andrew, "So What Really Changed after Enron?" *Corporate Reputation Review*, vol. 7.1, Spring 2004, pp. 55–63.

Ley, Janet, "Is This Telecom Armageddon?" *Business Communications Review*, vol. 36.5, May 2006, p. 13.

Linsky, Marty, "The Morning Meeting: Best-Practice Communication for Executive Teams," *Harvard Management Communication Letter*, vol. 3.2, Spring 2006, pp. 3–5.

Lopez, Chuck, "Admiral Dewey and the Art of Communication," *Industrial Management*, vol. 30.3, May/June 1988, p. 1.

Mai, Robert, and Alan Akerson, *The Leader as Communicator*, AMACOM, New York, 2003.

McKenzie, E. C. (Ed.). *14,000 Quips & Quotes for Writers & Speakers*, Greenwich House, New York, 1980.

Messmer, Max, "Managing Conflict," *Business Credit*, vol. 108.4, Apr. 2006, pp. 52–53.

Payne, Dinah, Cecily Raiborn, and Brenda Joyner, "How to be a Good Global Communicator," *The Journal of Corporate Accounting and Finance*, vol. 16.6, Sept./Oct. 2005, pp. 19–28.

Pearce, Terry, *Leading Out Loud*, Jossey-Bass, San Francisco, 2003.

Peverley, Phil, "The Politics of Politeness," *Pulse*, vol. 66.23, June 8, 2006, pp. 24–25.

Pomeroy, Ann, "Leaders Step Up Communication Efforts," *HR Magazine*, vol. 50.11, Nov. 2005, pp. 14, 16.

"Reasons Why Communication Fails," *Business Communicator*, vol. 5.7, Dec. 2004, p. 6.

Rice, F., "Champions of Communication," *Fortune*, vol. 123.11, June 3, 1991, pp. 111–112, 116, 120.

Riley, John, "Communication Key to Britannia Success," *Computer Weekly*, June 28, 2005, p. 6.

Rodenbough, Dean, "Building a Culture of Continuous Measurement at Hallmark," *Business Communicator*, vol. 5.10, Apr. 2005, pp. 10–11.

Schlegelmilch, Bodo B., and Irene Pollach., "The Perils and Opportunities of Communicating Corporate Ethics," *Journal of Marketing Management*, vol. 21.3, Apr. 2005, pp. 267–290.

Scoble, Robert, and Shel Israel, *Naked Conversations*, Wiley, Hoboken, N.J., 2006.

Sinickas, Angela, "Avoiding Global Misunderstandings," *Strategic Communication Management*, vol. 8.2, Feb./Mar. 2004, pp. 12–13.

Smithers, Chris, "Improving Communication to Boost Sales at BT," *Strategic Communication Management*, vol. 10.1, Dec. 2005/Jan. 2006, pp. 18–21.

Soll, Roger, " 'Sorry' Seen as a Magic Word to Avoid Suits," *Pediatrics*, vol. 115.2, Feb. 2005, p. 434.

Stapleton, Renee D., "Clinician Statements and Family Satisfaction with Family Conferences in the Intensive Care Unit," *Critical Care Medicine*, vol. 34.6, June 2006, pp. 1679–1685.

"Survey: Employees Want to Hear Information from the Top," *Public Relations Strategist*, vol. 11.4, Fall 2005, p. 4.

Thatcher, Mandy, "Challenging the Status Quo in Senior Leader Communication," *Strategic Communication Management*, vol. 9.6, Oct./Nov. 2005, p. 2.

Turley, Tim, "Be Understood II," *Embedded Systems Design*, vol. 18.12, Dec. 2005, pp. 5–9.

Waters, Meg, "Walk the Talk," *Business Performance Management*, vol. 3.3, Sept. 2005, p. 2.

Watson, Don, *Death Sentences*, Penguin Group, New York, 2005.

"Workers, Managers Not Aligned with Strategy," *T+D*, vol. 59.11, Nov. 2005, pp. 13–15.

Yates, Kathryn, "Internal Communication Effectiveness Enhances Bottom-Line Results," *Journal of Organizational Excellence*, vol. 25.3, Summer 2006, pp. 71–79.

Yaun, David, "Driving Culture Change by Consensus at IBM," *Strategic Communication Management*, vol. 10.3, Apr./May 2006, pp. 14–17.

Resources by Dianna Booher
Available from Booher Consultants

Books: Selected Titles

Communicate with Confidence®: How to Say It Right the First Time and Every Time

Speak with Confidence: Powerful Presentations That Inform, Inspire, and Persuade

E-Writing: 21st Century Tools for Effective Communication

From Contact to Contract: 496 Proven Sales Tips to Generate More Leads, Close More Deals, Exceed Your Goals, and Make More Money

Writing for Technical Professionals

Good Grief, Good Grammar

Great Personal Letters for Busy People: 501 Ready-to-Use Letters for Every Occasion

To the Letter: A Handbook of Model Letters for the Busy Executive

The Complete Letterwriter's Almanac

Winning Sales Letters

Executive's Portfolio of Model Speeches for All Occasions

The New Secretary: How to Handle People as Well as You Handle Paper

Clean Up Your Act: Effective Ways to Organize Paperwork and Get It Out of Your Life

Get a Life without Sacrificing Your Career

Your Signature Work: Creating Excellence and Influencing Others at Work

Your Signature Life: Pursuing God's Best Every Day

Ten Smart Moves for Women

Get Ahead, Stay Ahead

The Worth of a Woman's Words

Well Connected: Power Your Own Soul by Plugging into Others

Fresh-Cut Flowers for a Friend

The Little Book of Big Questions: Answers to Life's Perplexing Questions

Mother's Gifts to Me

The Esther Effect

Love Notes: From My Heart to Yours

First Thing Monday Morning

E-Learning Programs

Selling Skills and Strategies: Write Proposals That Win the Business

Selling Skills and Strategies: Thinking on Your Feet: Handling 11 Difficult Question Types

Selling Skills and Strategies: Write to Your Buyers: Email, Letters, Reports

Selling Skills and Strategies: Create and Deliver Sales Presentations with Impact

Selling Skills and Strategies: Negotiate So That Everyone Wins

Selling Skills and Strategies: Everyone Sells: Selling Skills for the Non-Salesperson

Selling Skills and Strategies: Manage Your Pipeline, Accounts, and Time

Effective Writing

Effective Editing

Good Grief, Good Grammar

More Good Grief, Good Grammar
Ready, Set, NeGOtiate

Workshops

Presentations That Work®
Strategic Writing™
Technical Writing
Developing Winning Proposals
Good Grief, Good Grammar
eService Communications
Communicate with Confidence®
Customer Service Communications
Listening until You Really Hear
Resolving Conflict Without Punching Someone Out
Meetings: Leading and Participating Productively
Negotiating So That Everyone Wins
E-mail Excellence™
Managing Information Overload: Increasing Your Personal Productivity

For More Information

For more information, please contact:

Booher Consultants, Inc.
2051 Hughes Rd.
Grapevine, TX 76051
Phone: (817) 318-6000
mailroom@booher.com
www.booher.com
www.BooherDirect.com
www.BooherBanter.typepad.com

Index

About the Author

Dianna Booher, CSP, CPAE, is an internationally recognized business communication expert and the author of 43 books published in 23 foreign editions. Numerous videos, audios, and Web-based e-learning systems based on her books help people improve communication, sales effectiveness, and productivity. She is the founder and president of Booher Consultants, Inc., based in the Dallas–Fort Worth Metroplex.

Since 1980, Booher Consultants has been helping executives, managers, and other professionals in organizations around the world to communicate what they mean clearly, concisely, and effectively. Their programs target all forms of corporate communication:

- written documents (e-mail, proposals, reports, letters, procedures),
- oral presentations
- meetings
- personal one-on-one interactions with colleagues, strategic partners, and customers.

Booher's approach to corporate and personal effectiveness focuses on the essential business communication skills that have universal application and are necessary for success in any industry or profession.

The firm provides communication consulting and training to some of the largest Fortune 500 companies and government agencies in the country, among them: Lockheed Martin, IBM, Dell, Lyondell Chemical, Siemens, Lucent Technologies, USAA, Bank of America, Verizon, Merrill Lynch, Principal Financial, State Farm Insurance, BP, Northwestern Mutual, J.P. Morgan Chase, Caterpillar, PepsiCo, Frito-Lay, Bayer, Nokia, JC Penney, the U.S. Navy, the Army and Air Force Exchange Service, the Library of Congress, the U.S. Department of Veterans Affairs, the U.S. Navy, and NASA.

Successful Meetings magazine has recognized Dianna in its list of "21 Top Speakers for the 21st Century." She has also won the highest awards in her industry, having been inducted into the National Speakers Association's Speaker Hall of Fame. Dianna earned a master's degree in English from the University of Houston.

For more information about bringing the Booher team into your organization to help you meet your own communication challenges, visit www.booher.com or call (800) 342-6621.